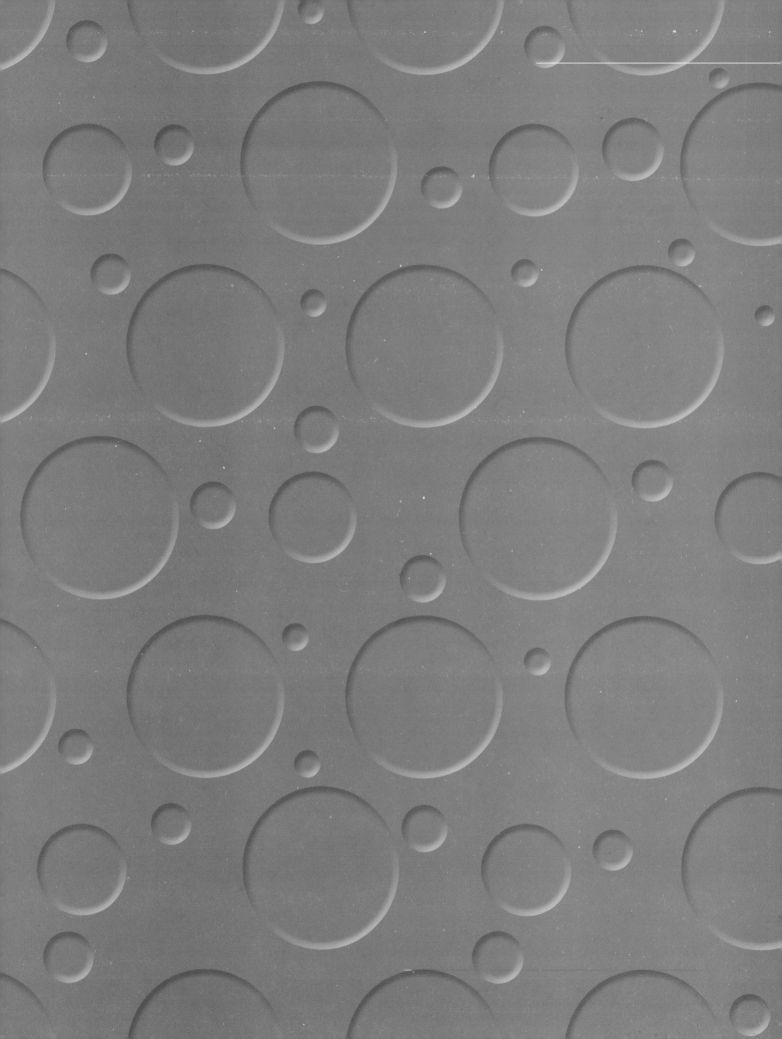

Harcourt Health and Fitness

 **Harcourt**

SCHOOL PUBLISHERS

Orlando • Austin • New York • San Diego • Toronto • London

Visit *The Learning Site!*
www.harcourtschool.com

CONSULTING AUTHORS

Lisa Bunting, M.Ed.
Physical Education Teacher
Katy Independent School District
Houston, Texas

Thomas M. Fleming, Ph.D.
Health and Physical Education
  Consultant
Austin, Texas

Charlie Gibbons, Ed.D.
Director, Youth and School Age
  Programs
Maxwell Air Force Base, Alabama
Former Adjunct Professor,
  Alabama State University
Health, Physical Education and
  Dance Department
Montgomery, Alabama

Jan Marie Ozias, Ph.D., R.N.
Director, Texas Diabetes Council;
  and Consultant, School Health
  Programs
Austin, Texas

Carl Anthony Stockton, Ph.D.
Dean, School of Education
The University of Texas at
  Brownsville and Texas
  Southmost College
Brownsville, Texas
Former Department Chair and
  Professor of Health Education
Department of Health and
  Applied Human Sciences
The University of North Carolina
  at Wilmington
Wilmington, North Carolina

Printed in the United States of America

ISBN 0-15-337524-8

3 4 5 6 7 8 9 10 032 13 12 11 10 09 08 07 06 05

Chapters

Contents

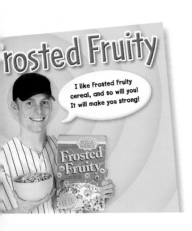

Why should you learn about health?

You can do many things to help yourself stay healthy and fit. You can also avoid doing things that will harm you. If you know ways to stay safe and healthy and do these things, you can help yourself have good health.

Staying active

Eating right

Getting enough rest

LIFE SKILLS

Why should you learn about life skills?

Being healthy and fit does not come from just knowing facts. You also have to think about these facts. You have to know how to use them every day.

These are some important life skills for you to have:

Making Decisions
Choosing the best thing to do

I think I'm sick. My stomach hurts.

Communicating
Sharing ideas, needs, and feelings with others

Managing Stress
Finding ways to help yourself relax

Refusing
Saying NO to things that can hurt you

Resolving Conflicts
Finding ways to solve problems that let both sides win

Setting Goals
Deciding on ways to improve your health and fitness

Whenever you see ![LIFE SKILLS] in this book, you can learn more about using life skills.

Why should you learn about good character?

Having good character is also an important part of having good health. When you have good character, you have good relationships with others. You can make good decisions about your health and fitness.

These are some important character traits:

Citizenship

Having pride in your school and community and obeying rules and laws

Caring

Showing kindness to friends, family, and others

Fairness

Treating others equally, playing by the rules, and being a good sport

Respect
Being considerate of yourself and others

Responsibility
Doing what you are supposed to do

Honesty
Telling the truth so others can trust you

Whenever you see **Building Good Character** in this book, you can learn more about building good character.

What are ways to be a successful reader?

You need good reading skills to do well in school. Here are some tips to help you understand, remember, and use information you read.

Reading Tip
This section tells you what the lesson is about.

Reading Tip
Vocabulary words are listed at the beginning of the lesson. They are also highlighted and defined when they are first used.

LESSON
1

Lesson Focus
Follow rules to stay safe at home and at school.

Vocabulary
emergency
playground
equipment

Staying Safe at Home and School

You and your family can make your home a safe place. Follow your family's safety rules. Put things away. Do not touch things that get hot.

BRIGHT

106

Answer this question to check how well you understood the lesson.

Whenever you see  in this book, you can learn more about using reading skills.

You can stay safe when you know what to do in an emergency. An **emergency** is a time when you need help right away. Call 911 in an emergency.

How is this family being safe?

107

Throughout **Harcourt Health and Fitness**, you will be able to learn new ideas and skills that will lead to good health.

You Are Growing

Make Predictions

When you make a prediction, you tell what you think will happen next.

> Prediction
>
> What Happened

Health Graph

My Family

babies	I
children	I I I I
adults	I I

Daily Physical Activity

You should exercise every day. It helps you take care of your body and its many parts.

Be Active! Use **Saucy Salsa** on Track 1.

Your Senses

People have five senses. The five **senses** are sight, hearing, smell, taste, and touch. You use different body parts for different senses.

see

smell

taste

hear

touch

You use your senses every day.
What senses is this girl using?

Your senses help you find out about the world. They help you learn. Senses also help you stay safe. They help you enjoy the things around you, too.

How are these people using their senses?

Review

1 **Vocabulary** What are your five **senses**?

2 What body parts do you use to see?

3 Write one way you use each of your senses.

Your Body Is Growing

Your body grows and changes in many ways. You **grow** when you become taller and heavier.

Once you were a baby. Now you are a child. One day you will be an adult.

All living things grow and change. People, animals, and plants are all living things.

What living things do you see here? How have they grown and changed?

Review

❶ **Vocabulary** What happens when you **grow**?

❷ Name one way you have grown or changed.

❸ Make a prediction. Draw what you think you might look like as an adult.

Your Body Moves

Your body has many bones. The bones make up your **skeleton**. Some bones hold up your body. Other bones protect parts inside your body.

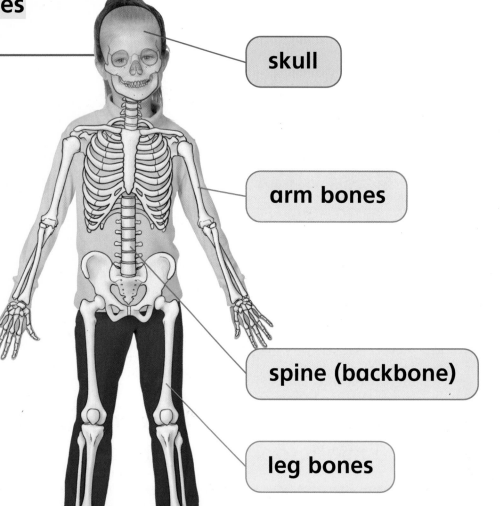

skull

arm bones

spine (backbone)

leg bones

Your **muscles** are body parts that help you move. They work together to move bones. One muscle pulls a bone one way. Another muscle pulls it back.

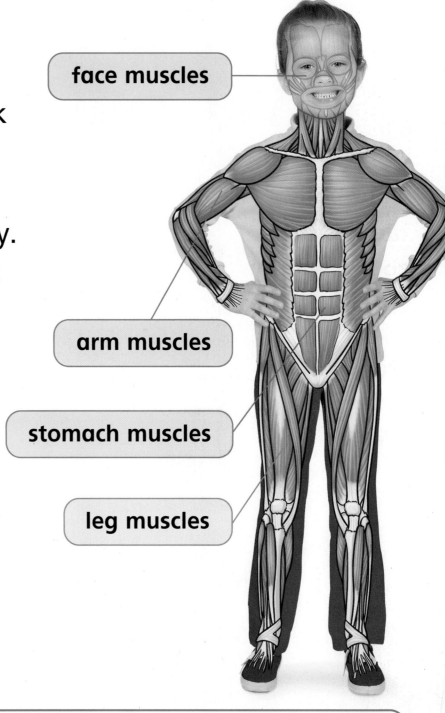

face muscles

arm muscles

stomach muscles

leg muscles

Review

1 **Vocabulary** What does your **skeleton** do?

2 What do your muscles do?

3 Write about what you might look like without bones.

How Your Body Digests Food

Energy is the power your body needs to do things. You digest food to get energy from it. **Digest** means to break down food.

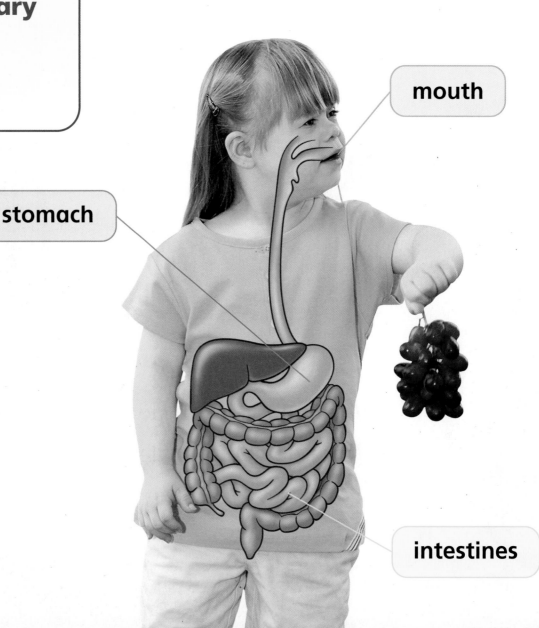

mouth

stomach

intestines

You start to digest food in your mouth. Your teeth tear food into small pieces.

Your tongue is a strong muscle. It helps you swallow food. It also helps you taste.

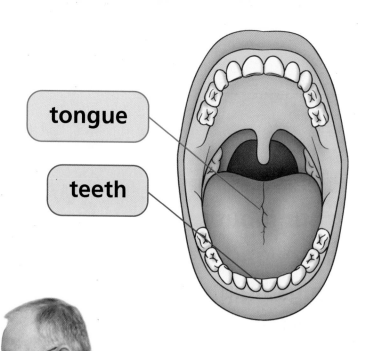

tongue

teeth

Review

1 **Vocabulary** Why does your body **digest** food?

2 What does your tongue do?

3 Draw a picture that shows where your body starts to digest food.

How You Breathe

Lesson Focus
Your mouth, nose, and lungs help you breathe.

Vocabulary
lungs

When you breathe, air goes in and out of your body. Your nose and mouth take in air. Then the air moves to your lungs. Your **lungs** take what your body needs from the air.

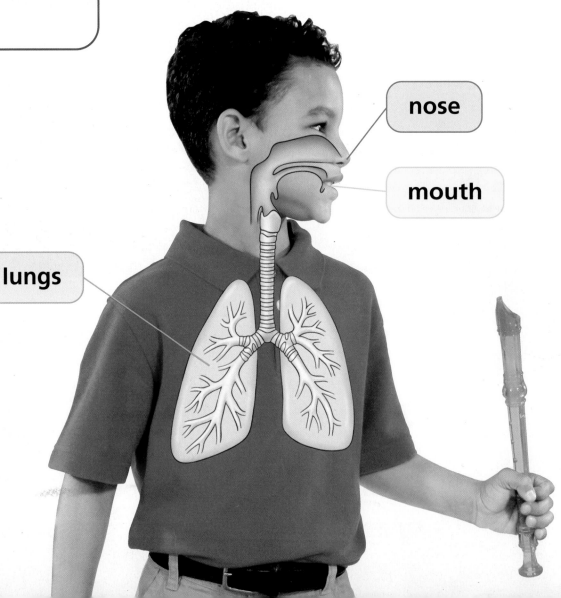

nose

mouth

lungs

Air leaves your lungs when you breathe out. The air moves back out through your nose and mouth.

Review

1 **Vocabulary** What do your **lungs** do?

2 Name all the body parts you use to breathe.

3 Write about what happens when you breathe. Draw a picture of your lungs.

How Your Blood Moves

Lesson Focus
Your heart and blood vessels move blood through your body.

Vocabulary
heart
blood vessels

Your heart and blood vessels move your blood through your body. Your **heart** is a muscle that pumps blood. Your **blood vessels** are tubes that carry blood.

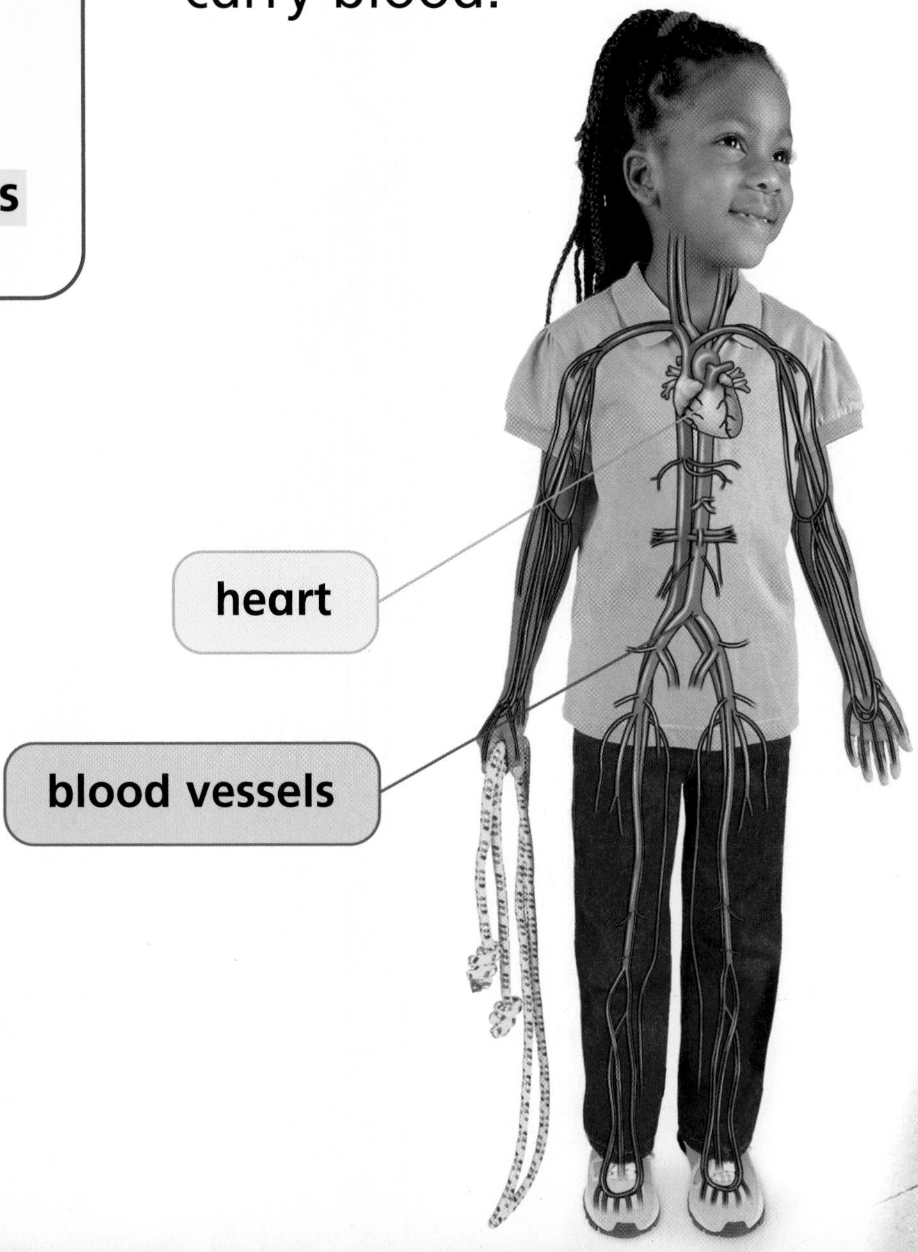

heart

blood vessels

Your heart pumps blood each time it beats. Your heart beats faster and works harder when you exercise. This hard work makes your heart strong.

Review

1 **Vocabulary** What do **blood vessels** do?

2 How does exercise help your heart?

3 Write what you can do to keep your heart healthy. Make a poster.

Set Goals

Setting a **goal** is choosing something to work for. You can set a goal to stay active.

1 **Set a goal.**

Lin sets a goal. He wants to stay active.

2 **Make a plan to meet the goal.**

Lin will exercise to meet his goal. He will run or ride his bike.

3 Work toward the goal.

Lin follows his plan. Today he chooses to run.

4 Ask yourself how you are doing.

Lin uses a chart to keep track of what he does. It helps him meet his goal to stay active.

 Problem Solving

Use the steps to solve this problem.

You want to stay active. What can you do to meet this goal?

 **Math**

Favorite Smells Table

How many children like to smell apples?

What do the most children like to smell?

Make a graph using the numbers from the tally table.

Favorite Smells	
flowers	|||||
apples	||
bread baking	|||

 Writing

Your Life Story

Draw pictures of yourself at different ages. What could you do at each age? Write about it. Make a book with your pictures. Share it with others.

My Life

 GO ONLINE For more activities, visit The Learning Site.
www.harcourtschool.com/health

Honesty

Being Honest About Your Health

Your parents may ask about your health. They may ask how you care for your body.

Be honest with your parents about your health. Being **honest** is telling the truth. This will help your parents get you the care you need.

This girl does not feel well. How is she being honest about her health?

Activity

Draw a picture of the last time you visited the doctor. Write about how you were honest about your health.

Chapter Review

Use Health Words

Use each word to tell about the picture.

1 senses

2 digest

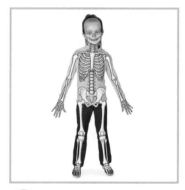

3 skeleton

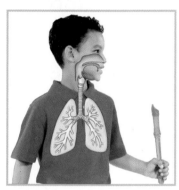

4 lungs

(Focus Skill) Reading Skill

5 Make a prediction. How will the baby on page 8 grow and change? Look at the rest of page 8 for clues.

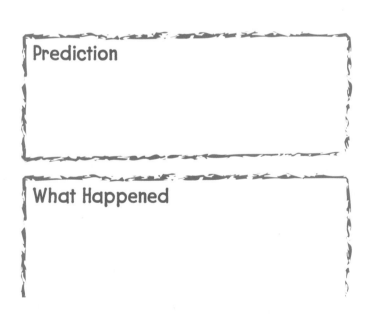

Prediction

What Happened

Use Life Skills

Look at the pictures. Then answer the questions.

6 Which picture shows Lin keeping track of his exercise goal?

7 What are four steps that can help you set goals?

Write About It

8 Draw a picture of your body. Show where your heart is. Write a sentence that tells what it does.

My heart pumps blood.

CHAPTER 2

Taking Care of Your Body

Use Context Clues

The words, pictures, and charts near a new word can help you read and understand it.

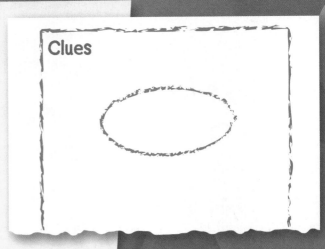

Clues

Health Graph

How Many Ads?

shampoo

toothpaste

soap

0 1 2 3

Daily Physical Activity

Keeping clean helps you stay healthy. Exercise helps you stay healthy too.

 **Be Active!**
Use **Get On Board** on Track 2.

Caring for Your Skin

Lesson Focus
Caring for your skin helps you stay healthy.

Vocabulary
germs
sunburn
sunscreen

Keeping clean helps you stay healthy. Soap and water help wash away germs. **Germs** are tiny things that can make you sick. You can get germs from pets and other things you touch.

Wash your hands before and after you eat. Wash your hands often during the day.

Why is this girl washing her
hands?

Protect your skin from the sun. The sun can make your skin red and sore. This is called **sunburn**.

Wear sunscreen when you are outside. **Sunscreen** helps protect your skin from the sun. The sun can harm your skin even on a cloudy day.

In the Sun

► Wear sunscreen with SPF 30 or higher.

► Wear clothes that cover your skin.

► Wear a hat and sunglasses.

► Find shade if you feel hot.

► Drink water.

Review

1. **Vocabulary** What are **germs**?

2. When should you wear sunscreen?

3. Draw a picture. Show how you keep your skin healthy.

Health-Care Products and Ads

Lesson Focus
Choose the health-care products that are best for you.

Vocabulary
ad

Some products can help you stay healthy. Choose the best products for you. Ask an adult to read the labels. Labels tell what products do and what is in them. Labels can help you tell how products are alike and different.

An **ad** is a message that tries to get you to buy something. Some ads do not tell you all you need to know.

Look for products that have what you need. Look for products that have good prices.

SMILE BRIGHT
Toothpaste
will make your teeth
WHITE AND
BRIGHT!

Brighten your smil
with this money sa

SMILE BRIGHT
Toothpaste
50¢ OF
any size

Shiny!

Children's Body Wash

FRESH'N'WHITE Toothpaste

You will love your smile! Get a FREE toothbrush too!

FRESH'N'WHITE Toothpaste

Buy FRESH'N'WHITE and get a FREE toothbrush too!

Review

1 **Vocabulary** What does an **ad** try to do?

2 What should you ask an adult to read before you buy something?

3 Write an ad for soap. Tell why people should buy it.

People to Ask for Health Information

Lesson Focus
You can find health information in many places.

You may have questions about your health. Talk to your parents or other trusted adults. Talk to your doctor or other health-care workers.

You can find health information in books and videos. You can use a computer. Always ask a parent or teacher to help you.

Review

1. Who can you ask for health information?

2. Where can you look to find an answer to a health question?

3. Write to tell others where they can find health information. Make a poster.

Set Goals

Set a goal to choose the best health-care products. Choosing the best products can help you stay healthy.

1 **Set a goal.**

Jill is going to the pool. Her goal is to choose the right sunscreen. It must protect her from sunburn.

2 **Make a plan to meet the goal.**

Jill asks her mother for help. They look at the labels. They talk about how the sunscreens are different.

3 Work toward the goal.

One sunscreen has a higher SPF. It blocks the sun better. Jill chooses the better sunscreen.

4 Ask yourself how you are doing.

Jill puts on her sunscreen often. She does not get a sunburn.

Problem Solving

Use the steps to solve this problem.

You want to keep clean. Your goal is to choose the right soap. How can you meet this goal?

Math

Sun Protection Graph

What did the child use most often?

What did the child use least often?

Make your own graph about sun protection.

My Sun Protection This Week

sunscreen	🧴	🧴	🧴	🧴
hat	👒	👒		
sunglasses	👓			

Writing

Health Poster

Make a poster about washing hands. Explain how washing hands helps people stay healthy. Share your poster with your class.

Washing your hands helps you stay healthy.

 For more activities, visit The Learning Site.
www.harcourtschool.com/health

Honesty

Being an Honest Consumer

Be honest when you shop for health products. Tell someone if you break a product in a store. Do not return a product if you break it after you use it.

You may find that a product is broken before you use it. Then you should return it to the store.

What are other ways you can be honest when you shop for products?

Activity

Look at this picture. Act out ways to be honest.

39

Chapter Review

Use Health Words

Tell which picture goes best with the word.

1 **sunburn**

2 **ad**

3 **germs**

4 **sunscreen**

a.

b.

c.

d.

Focus Skill **Reading Skill**

5 Read the context clues in the box. Use them to figure out the missing word in the center.

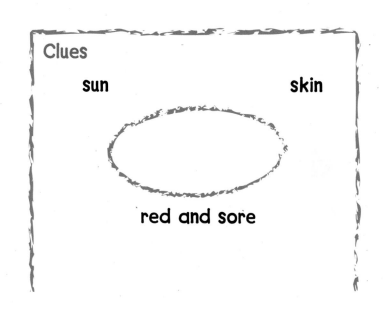

Clues

sun   skin

red and sore

Use Life Skills

Look at the pictures. Then answer the questions.

6 Jill set a goal to choose the right sunscreen. Which picture shows that Jill met her goal?

7 What four steps can help you set goals to choose good products?

I wash my hands with soap. Washing helps take the germs away.

Write About It

8 Draw a picture that shows one way you take care of your body. Write about why this is important.

Your Teeth

Sequence
When you sequence things, you put them in the order in which they happened.

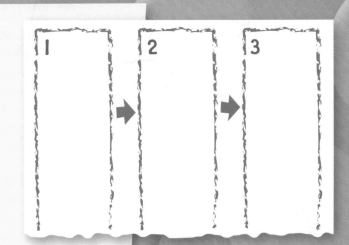

Health Graph

Favorite Toothpaste Flavors

mint

cinnamon

fruit

0 1 2 3

Daily Physical Activity

Brush and floss your teeth every day. You should also exercise every day.

 **Be Active!**
Use **Late for Supper** on Track 3.

Your Teeth

You use your teeth when you eat. You have different kinds of teeth. They help you do different things.

Your front teeth are sharp.
They help you bite into food.
Your back teeth are wide.
They help you chew food into
small pieces.

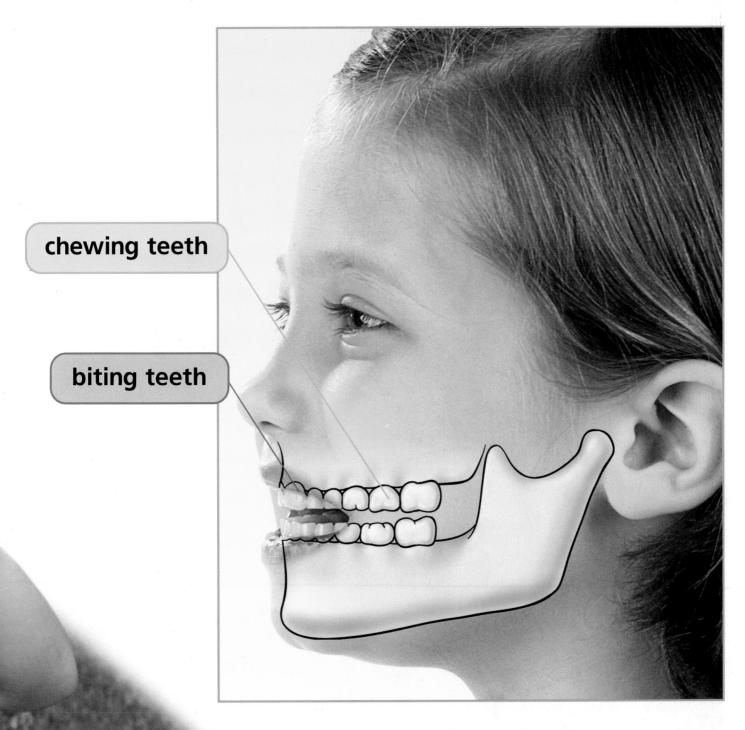

chewing teeth

biting teeth

Your first teeth are called **primary teeth**. Primary teeth grow in when you are a baby. You lose these teeth when you are about your age. Soon new teeth begin to grow in.

Your new teeth are called **permanent teeth**. They are bigger. They fit you when you grow up. Take good care of these teeth. You will have them for the rest of your life.

Taking Care of Your Teeth

Lesson Focus
Brushing and using floss keeps your teeth clean and healthy.

Vocabulary
floss

Brushing helps keep your teeth clean and healthy. Brush your teeth in the morning. Brush them before you go to bed. Brush them after you eat.

Use a soft toothbrush that is the right size for you. Put toothpaste the size of a pea on the brush. Brush your teeth. Then rinse your mouth with water.

❶ Brush the outsides of all of your teeth.

❷ Brush the insides of all of your teeth.

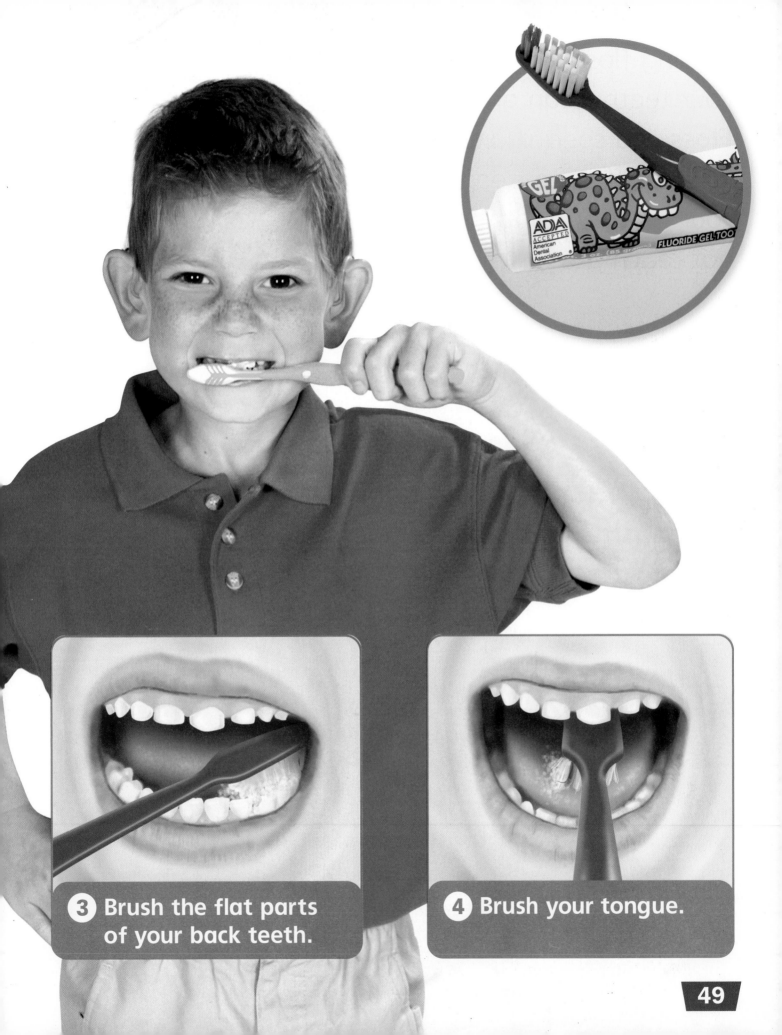

3 Brush the flat parts of your back teeth.

4 Brush your tongue.

49

Using floss also helps keep your teeth clean and healthy. **Floss** is a special kind of thread. You use floss to clean between your teeth. A toothbrush will not reach there.

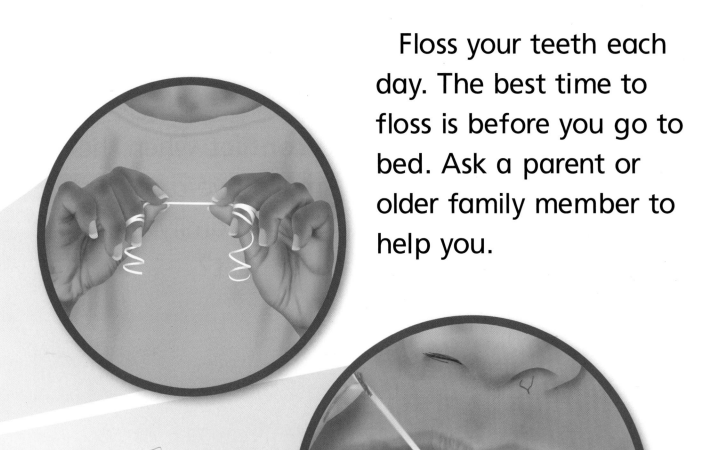

Floss your teeth each day. The best time to floss is before you go to bed. Ask a parent or older family member to help you.

Review

1. **Vocabulary** Why do you need to use **floss**?

2. When should you brush your teeth?

3. Write to tell others why they should brush and floss their teeth. Make a poster.

Resolve Conflicts

People have a **conflict** when they do not agree. You may have a conflict with someone in your family. How can you resolve your conflict?

1 **Agree that there is a problem.**

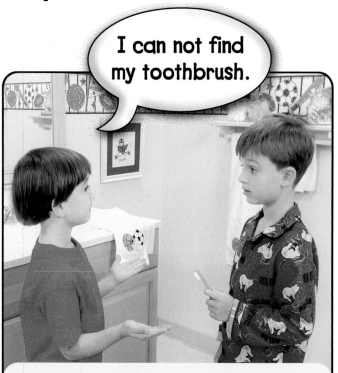

I can not find my toothbrush.

Tim can not find his toothbrush. He wants to use Joel's toothbrush.

2 **Listen to each other.**

No! Do not use my toothbrush.

Joel says no. He knows sharing it would mean sharing germs. Tim gets angry with Joel.

3 Think of ways to work together.

You may use this toothbrush.

Joel has a better idea. He finds a new toothbrush. He gives it to Tim.

4 Find a way for both sides to win.

Each boy uses his own toothbrush. Now they both have clean teeth.

 Problem Solving

Use the steps to solve this problem.

You and your sister want to brush your teeth at the same time. Your sister does not want to share the sink. How do you resolve your conflict?

Keeping Your Teeth Safe

You need your teeth to eat. This is why you should keep them safe. Never use your teeth for anything but eating. You do not want to break them.

You can protect your teeth when you play sports. Wear a mouth guard. It will help keep your teeth safe.

Review

1 What do you need your teeth for?

2 How can you keep your teeth safe?

3 Draw a picture. Show a child doing something that could harm his or her teeth. Mark an X over the picture.

Going to the Dentist

Dentists are people who care for teeth. They check to make sure your teeth are healthy. Dentists will fix any tooth problems you may have.

Always cooperate when a dentist is checking your teeth.

Dental hygienists also care for teeth. They help the dentist by cleaning your teeth.

Dentists and dental hygienists help you take good care of your teeth. They show you how to care for them. Be sure to follow their instructions.

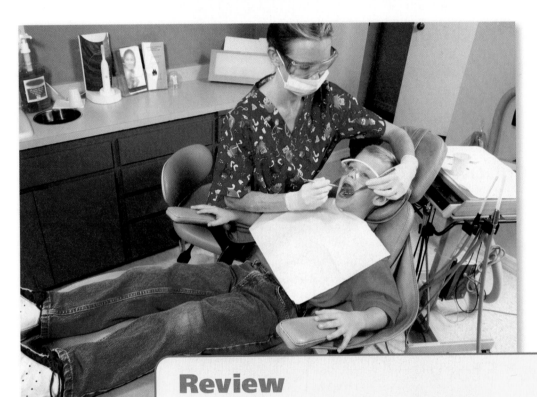

Review

1. **Vocabulary** What do **dentists** do?

2. Why is it important to cooperate when a dentist or dental hygienist is cleaning your teeth?

3. Write a question about your teeth that you could ask a dentist.

ACTIVITIES

Math

Missing Teeth Graph

Who is missing the most teeth?

What is the difference between the most and fewest?

Make your own graph about teeth.

Writing

A Dentist Story

Draw a picture of yourself visiting the dentist. How does he or she care for your teeth? Write about it.

GO ONLINE For more activities, visit The Learning Site.
www.harcourtschool.com/health

Responsibility

Taking Care of Your Teeth

Taking care of your teeth is your responsibility. A **responsibility** is something you need to do on your own.

You can take responsibility by brushing and flossing your teeth each day on your own. Your parents should not need to tell you to do this.

How is this girl taking responsibility?

Activity

Draw pictures to show how you take responsibility.

Chapter Review

Use Health Words

Tell which picture goes best with the word or words.

1 **primary teeth**

2 **permanent teeth**

3 **floss**

4 **dentist**

a.

b.

c.

d.

Focus Skill Reading Skill

5 Sequence the pictures by numbering them in order.

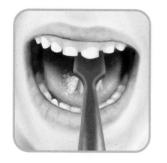

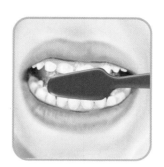

Use Life Skills

Look at the pictures. Then answer the questions.

6 Which picture shows how the boys worked together?

7 What are four steps that can help you resolve conflicts?

Write About It

8 Write about what would happen if you did not brush and floss your teeth.

Food would stay on my teeth and harm them.

CHAPTER 4 Wonderful Food

62

Reading Skill

Find the Main Idea

The main idea of something you are reading is what it is mostly about. The details tell more about it.

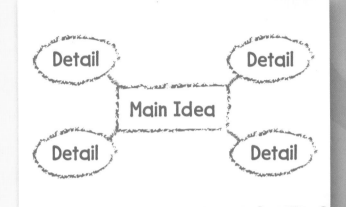

Detail

Detail

Main Idea

Detail

Detail

Health Graph

Our Favorite Snacks

3

2

1

0

apples | bananas | granola bars

Daily Physical Activity

Eat foods that are good for you. Exercise every day.

**Be Active!**
Use **Jam and Jive** on Track 4.

You Need Food

Food helps your body grow and stay healthy. Food also gives you energy. Energy is the power your body needs to do things.

Look at the ways these children are using energy. How do you use energy each day?

Review

1. What is energy?

2. Why does your body need food?

3. Write a list of some ways you use energy every day.

Food Guide Pyramid

Lesson Focus

The Food Guide Pyramid can help you choose foods.

Vocabulary

Food Guide Pyramid

fats, sweets, and oils

milk, yogurt, and cheese

vegetables

breads, cereals, rice, and pasta

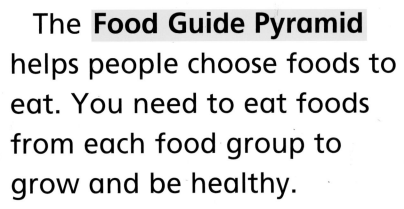

The **Food Guide Pyramid** helps people choose foods to eat. You need to eat foods from each food group to grow and be healthy.

Look at the pyramid. The food group at the bottom is the largest. Eat more foods from this group and fewer from the top.

meat, poultry, fish, dried beans, eggs, and nuts

fruits

Most meals are made of foods from more than one group. What foods are used to make a taco? Which groups are the foods in the taco from?

Which food groups are these foods from?

Review

1. **Vocabulary** How can the **Food Guide Pyramid** help you?

2. From which part of the pyramid should you eat the most foods?

3. Draw a meal you would like to eat. Show foods from all the groups.

Choosing Foods for Meals and Snacks

Eating a meal is a good way to get foods from many food groups. **Breakfast**, **lunch**, and **dinner** are three meals that many people eat every day.

A good breakfast gives your body the energy it needs to start the day. A good lunch and dinner help your body have energy all day long.

Breakfast

Lunch

Dinner

When you feel hungry between meals, you might want to eat a snack. A **snack** is food you eat between meals. Snacks give you extra energy for work and play. Choose healthful snacks from different food groups.

What snacks do you see in these pictures? What food groups do these snacks come from?

Review

1. **Vocabulary** How do **breakfast**, **lunch**, **dinner**, and **snacks** help you?

2. Why should you eat many kinds of foods?

3. Write a menu for three meals. Choose foods from all the groups.

Make Decisions

Making good choices about foods will help you stay healthy. How can you choose foods that will give you the energy you need?

1 **Think about the choices.**

2 **Say NO to choices that are against your family's rules.**

Al wants to choose a breakfast food. It must give his body energy for his soccer game.

Al knows that his parents do not want him to eat sweets for breakfast.

3 **Ask yourself what could happen with each choice.**

4 **Make the best choice.**

A bowl of cereal will give Al energy to play.

Al chooses cereal with low-fat milk, orange juice, and toast. He will have energy to play and have fun.

Problem Solving

Use the steps to solve this problem.

You want lunch. You can have a cheese sandwich, an apple, and low-fat milk. Or you can have a hot dog, chips, and a soda. Which lunch should you choose? Why?

Food Ads

An ad is a message that tries to get you to buy something. There are many ads on TV. An ad may use a song. It may show someone famous. It may even offer you a free toy.

Some ads make foods seem healthful when they really have too much sugar, fat, or salt.

You will love this sweet treat! You get a free toy, too!

How does this ad try to get you to buy Super Sweets? What do you need to know about Super Sweets?

Review

1 What does an ad try to do?

2 What should you watch and listen for in ads?

3 Write an ad for a healthful snack. Tell why people should eat it.

Handling Food Safely

You can help keep your foods safe to eat. Follow these rules.

► Wash your hands with soap and water before and after you touch foods.

► Wash fruits and vegetables in cold water.

► Cover foods and put them away.

► Some foods, such as milk, eggs, juice, and meat, must stay cold. Keep them in the refrigerator.

Review

1. Why is it important to handle foods safely?

2. What foods should you wash?

3. Write a list of foods. Tell how to keep each food safe.

ACTIVITIES

Math

Sorting Foods Graph

How many foods are green?

How many more foods are green than orange?

Sort foods by taste. Make a graph.

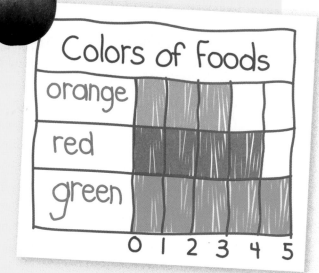

Colors of Foods

orange		
red		
green		

0 1 2 3 4 5

Writing

Write a Recipe

Write the recipe for a snack. Follow the recipe to prepare the snack. Handle foods safely. Try your snack.

Ants on a Log

1 piece of celery
peanut butter
6 raisins
Put peanut butter on
a piece of celery.
Put six raisins on
top of the peanut butter.

 For more activities, visit The Learning Site.
www.harcourtschool.com/health

Respect

Being Polite in the Lunchroom

You know that you should eat a healthful lunch. You will enjoy your lunch more if you and your friends are polite. Being **polite** is showing respect for others. It helps everyone feel safe and relaxed while eating.

How are these children being polite while they eat lunch?

Activity

Make a list of ways to be polite in the lunchroom.

Chapter Review

Use Health Words

Tell which picture goes best with the word or words.

1 breakfast

2 dinner

3 Food Guide Pyramid

4 snack

a.

b.

c.

d.

(Focus Skill) Reading Skill

5 Tell the main idea.

Detail
I can cover and put away foods.

Detail
I can put foods in the refrigerator.

Main Idea
I can help keep foods _____.

Detail
I can wash my hands.

Detail
I can wash fruits and vegetables.

Use Life Skills

Look at the picture. Then answer the questions.

6 Why did Al choose this meal?

7 What are four steps that can help you make decisions?

Write About It

8 Write a rhyme about foods.

Foods

I like eggs
And turkey legs,
Apples, cheese,
And little peas.

Keeping Active

Find Cause and Effect

An effect is something that happens. A cause is the reason something happens.

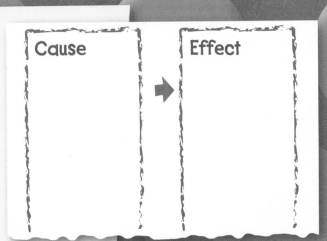

Cause		Effect
	→	

Health Graph

Time Bob Spent Exercising	
Sunday	☺ ☺ ☺ ☺
Monday	☺ ☺
Tuesday	☺ ☺ ☺
Wednesday	☺ ☺
Thursday	☺ ☺ ☺
Friday	☺ ☺
Saturday	☺ ☺ ☺

Key: Each ☺ stands for 10 minutes.

Daily Physical Activity

Exercise, healthful foods, and rest help you stay fit.

 **Be Active!** Use **Flexercise** on Track 5.

Good Posture

Posture is the way you hold your body. Have good posture when you sit. Keep your back straight. Hold your head up. Pull your shoulders back. Put your feet flat on the floor or on a footrest.

Have good posture when you stand or walk. Keep your back straight. Hold your head up. Pull your shoulders back.

Good posture helps your body grow straight. It helps you breathe better. It also helps you look your best.

Review

1 Vocabulary What is **posture**?

2 How can you have good posture?

3 Write about how good posture helps you.

Your Physical Fitness and Exercise

Lesson Focus
Exercise, healthful foods, and rest help you stay fit.

Vocabulary
physical fitness
exercise

Having **physical fitness** means having a strong and healthy body. Being fit helps you look and feel your best. To stay fit, you can exercise. **Exercise** is moving your body to make it work hard. Exercise is a way to have fun.

Eating healthful foods helps you stay fit. Choose foods that are good for your body.

Getting enough rest also helps you stay fit. Rest helps you feel your best.

Exercise helps your heart and lungs stay healthy. It makes your bones and muscles strong. It helps your body fight germs. Exercise helps you feel your best.

You can exercise in many ways.
How are these children exercising?
How do you like to exercise?

Review

1 **Vocabulary** What is **physical fitness**?

2 How does exercise help your body?

3 Write a list of your favorite ways to exercise.

Manage Stress

You may feel stress before a soccer game or a school play. **Stress** is a feeling of worry. What can you do to manage stress?

1 **Know what stress feels like.**

Sue will be in a school play tomorrow. She feels stress. Her head hurts. Her legs feel weak.

2 **Think about what is making you feel stress.**

Sue is afraid she will make mistakes on stage. She might forget her words. She might fall.

③ Do something that will help you feel better.

Sue walks her dog. Walking helps her forget her stress.

④ Get exercise.

Sue rides her bike. The fresh air and exercise make her feel better.

Problem Solving

Use the steps to solve this problem.

You will be in a T-ball game tomorrow. You are worried that you will not play well. What can you do to manage your stress?

Exercising Safely

You can keep your body safe when you exercise.

First, warm up your muscles. You can run in place or do jumping jacks. Stretch your muscles. To **stretch** is to gently pull your muscles. Then you will be ready to exercise safely.

1. Warm up.

Cool down after you exercise. Walk around until your heartbeat slows down. Take deep breaths. Stretch again. Stretch all the muscles you used while exercising.

2. Do the exercise.

3. Cool down.

Stay safe by wearing safety
gear. For some kinds of exercise,
you may need a helmet, a mouth
guard, wrist guards, and pads.

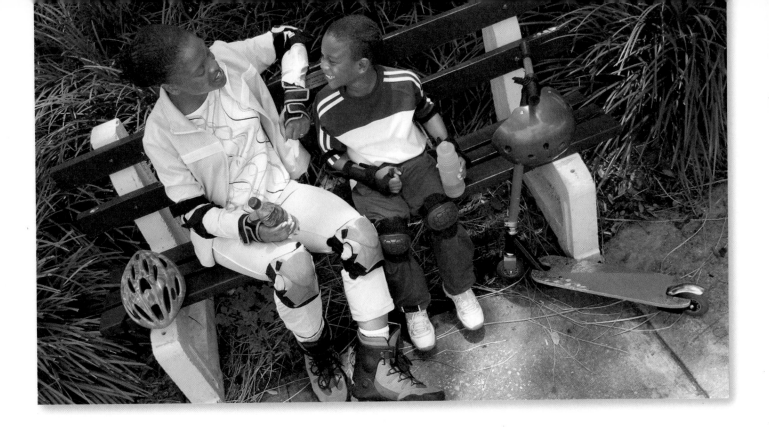

Safety Tips

► Warm up and cool down.

► Wear safety gear.

► Drink lots of water.

► Stop to rest.

► Watch the weather.

Review

1 **Vocabulary** When do you need to **stretch**?

2 What should you do before you exercise?

3 Write a safety guide. List tips for exercising safely.

You Need Sleep

You need sleep to stay healthy. Your body needs rest. A tired body has a harder time fighting germs. It also cannot grow well.

Getting enough sleep gives you energy to run and play. It helps you think and learn. You can do your best when you get enough sleep each night.

Review

1. Why do you need sleep?

2. Name two ways getting enough sleep helps you.

3. Write a sentence. Tell what might happen if you did not get enough sleep.

Math

Bike Helmet Graph

How many children have red helmets?

What color helmet do the fewest children have?

Make your own graph about safety equipment.

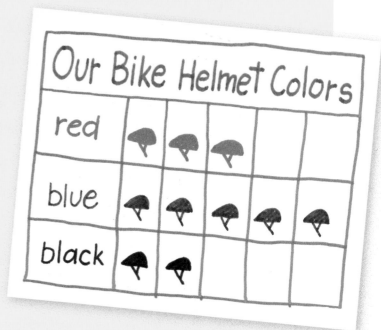

Writing

Safety Gear

Draw a picture of yourself dressed to exercise. What safety gear do you wear? Label each thing. Write a sentence that tells how one of them keeps you safe.

For more activities, visit The Learning Site.
www.harcourtschool.com/health

Fairness

Playing by the Rules

You show fairness when you play by the rules. **Fairness** means treating others the way you want them to treat you.

Follow the rules in games and sports. Take turns with others. Share toys. Be sure that there is a way for everyone to play.

How are these children showing fairness?

Activity

Write a list of rules for showing fairness when you play with others.

Chapter Review

Use Health Words

Use the words to tell about the pictures.

1 posture

2 exercise

3 stretch

(Focus Skill) Reading Skill

Tell two more causes for the effect.

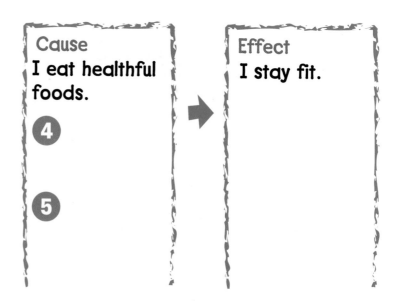

Cause	Effect
I eat healthful foods.	I stay fit.
4	
5	

Use Life Skills

Look at the pictures. Then answer the questions.

6 Which picture shows Sue doing something to forget her stress?

7 What are four steps you can use to manage stress?

Write About It

8 Write about one way you exercise. What do you do to stay safe when you exercise?

I jog. I stretch before I jog.

Being Safe

Reading Skill

Sequence

When you sequence things, you put them in the order in which they happen.

Health Graph

Water Sports

6
5
4
3
2
1
0

swimming | sailing | fishing

Daily Physical Activity

You should exercise every day. Follow the rules for safe exercise.

 **Be Active!**

Use **Muscle Mambo** on Track 6.

Staying Safe at Home and School

Lesson Focus

Follow rules to stay safe at home and at school.

Vocabulary

emergency
playground
equipment

You and your family can make your home a safe place. Follow your family's safety rules. Put things away. Do not touch things that get hot.

You can stay safe when you know what to do in an emergency. An **emergency** is a time when you need help right away. Call 911 in an emergency.

How is this family being safe?

Follow your school rules. They help you stay safe. Your teacher can tell you the rules for your class.

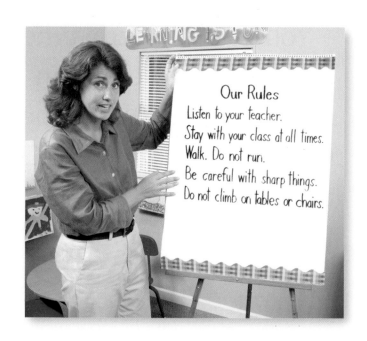

Our Rules
Listen to your teacher.
Stay with your class at all times.
Walk. Do not run.
Be careful with sharp things.
Do not climb on tables or chairs.

► Do not climb up a slide.

► Wait your turn.

► Go one at a time.

► Do not jump off the bars or swings.

► Do not walk in front of a moving swing.

Rules help you stay safe when you use the playground. Swings, slides, and bars are **playground equipment**. Follow the rules so that no one gets hurt.

Review

1 **Vocabulary** What is an **emergency**?

2 How can you stay safe at school?

3 Write rules for your school playground.

Car and Bus Safety

Lesson Focus
Follow rules
to stay safe
in a car or on
a bus.

Vocabulary
safety belt

You can follow rules to stay safe in a car. Sit in the back seat on a booster seat until you grow taller. Put on your safety belt before the car starts moving. A **safety belt** is a strap that holds you in your seat.

Stay safe while the car moves. Do not bother the driver. Sit still. Talk quietly. Keep your head and hands inside the car. Do not take off your safety belt.

Follow rules to stay safe when you wait for a bus. Wait for the bus in a safe place.

Wait for your turn to get on and off the bus. Do not push on the steps of the bus. To cross the street, walk in front of the bus.

Stay safe while the bus moves. Listen to your bus driver. Stay in your seat. Talk quietly. Do not stand up until the bus stops.

Review

1 **Vocabulary** When should you wear a **safety belt**?

2 How can you stay safe in a car?

3 Write a thank-you card to someone who safely drives you in a car or bus.

Staying Safe While Walking and Biking

You can stay safe when you cross a street. Choose a safe place to cross. A **crosswalk** is a place marked on the street where you can cross safely. Follow these four steps.

❶ Stop.

Do not walk into the street before you stop.

❷ Look.

Look left. Look right. Then look left again.

❸ Listen.

Sometimes you can hear things before you can see them. Do not cross if you hear something coming.

❹ Think.

Cross only when the street is clear. Look and listen as you cross. Cross quickly, but do not run.

You can be safe on a bike. Wear the right gear. Put a helmet on your head. Wear bright colors. Always wear shoes.

You also need a safe bike. It must be the right size. Check that it has all the parts shown below.

horn

reflectors

Stay safe while riding your bike. Ride in a line if you are with friends. Keep your hands on the handlebars. Walk your bike when you cross the street. Never ride at night.

Review

1. **Vocabulary** What is a **crosswalk**?

2. How can you ride a bike safely?

3. Write steps for crossing a street safely.

Fire Safety

You can stay safe from fires. Do not play with matches or lighters. They start fires. Fires can harm you, your family, and your home.

Stay away from anything that can get hot. Never cook without an adult. Do not touch electric cords, plugs, or outlets.

Know what to do if there is a fire. Make a plan with your family. Practice it. If there is a fire, leave your home quickly. Call 911 when you are out and safe.

smoke detector

Stop, drop, and roll if your clothes ever catch fire.

❶ Stop.

Do not run. Do not wave your arms.

❷ Drop.

Lie down quickly. Cover your face with your hands.

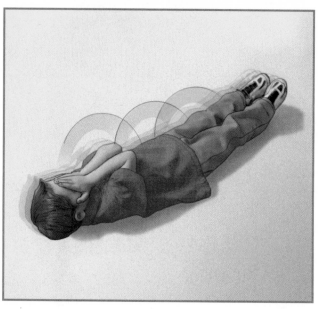

❸ Roll.

Roll over and over to put out the fire.

You have drills at school. Drills help you practice what to do if there is an emergency.

You leave the school for a fire drill. Follow the rules. Stay in line. Do not talk. Listen to your teacher.

Review

1. How can you stay safe from fires?

2. What should you do if your clothes catch fire?

3. Write a plan. Tell what you would do if there was a fire at your home.

LIFE SKILLS

Say NO and Stay Safe

Sometimes friends may want you to do unsafe things. You can stay safe by saying NO to them. Here is how.

1 **Say NO. Tell why not.**

Grace is at Ana's house. Ana wants to play with matches. Grace knows they should not.

2 **Think about what could happen.**

Grace says that they could start a fire. The fire could hurt them or burn Ana's home.

3 **Suggest something else to do.**

Grace thinks of a safe way to have fun. She says she and Ana could go play outside.

4 **Say NO again. Walk away.**

Oh, come on!

I said NO! Put the matches away, or I am going home.

Grace will not stay at Ana's house unless Ana puts the matches away.

Problem Solving

Use the steps to solve this problem.

You are at your friend's house. Your friend wants to cook on the kitchen stove. You know this is unsafe. How should you say NO?

Water Safety

Stay safe in or near water. You can get hurt if you are not careful. Follow all the rules for water safety. Then water can be fun for everyone.

1. Learn to swim.
2. Never swim alone.
3. Follow the rules.
4. Watch the weather.
5. Wear a life jacket.
6. In an emergency, call 911.

Watch the weather. Protect yourself from the sun. Get out of the water if you see lightning or hear thunder.

Follow the rules for boats. Wear a life jacket. Do not stand up in a boat.

Review

1 What should you do if you are in the water and hear thunder?

2 What do you need to wear in a boat?

3 Write rules for a pool. Tell others how to stay safe around water.

Math

Traffic Signs Graph

How many stop signs were seen?

How many more traffic lights were seen than school crossing signs?

Make your own graph about traffic signs.

Traffic Signs

stop sign					
traffic light					
school crossing sign					

Writing

Make a Safety Guide

How can people stay safe while riding bikes? Draw pictures that show how. Write about what people should do. Then make a book.

MY BIKE SAFETY GUIDE

GO **ONLINE** For more activities, visit The Learning Site. www.harcourtschool.com/health

Responsibility

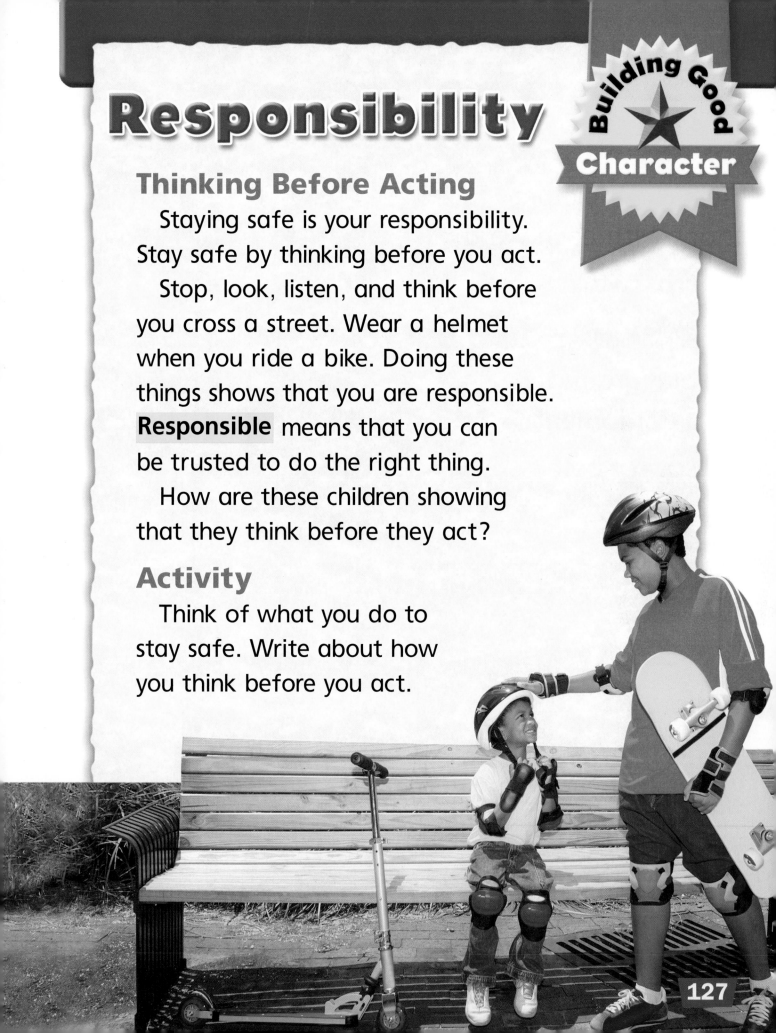

Building Good Character

Thinking Before Acting

Staying safe is your responsibility. Stay safe by thinking before you act.

Stop, look, listen, and think before you cross a street. Wear a helmet when you ride a bike. Doing these things shows that you are responsible. **Responsible** means that you can be trusted to do the right thing.

How are these children showing that they think before they act?

Activity

Think of what you do to stay safe. Write about how you think before you act.

Chapter Review

Use Health Words

Tell which picture goes with each word.

1. crosswalk
2. emergency
3. playground equipment
4. safety belt

a.

b.

c.

d.

Focus Skill Reading Skill

5. Sequence the pictures by numbering them in order.

Use Life Skills

Look at the picture. Then answer the questions.

6 Why should you say NO to playing with matches?

7 What are four steps you can use to say NO to unsafe things?

Write About It

8 Write a list of ways to stay safe while riding a bike. Then draw a bike, and label the parts that make it safe.

reflectors

horn

I can wear bright colors.

7 Avoiding Danger

Recall and Retell

To recall is to remember what you have read. To retell is to tell it in your own words.

Recall Detail	Retell
Recall Detail	
Recall Detail	

Health Graph

Trusted Adults at a Mall

police	🧍
guard	🧍 🧍
clerk	🧍 🧍 🧍

Key: Each 🧍 stands for 5 people.

Daily Physical Activity

You should exercise every day. To avoid danger, never exercise alone.

🎵 **Be Active!**

Use **Movin' and Groovin'** on Track 7.

Staying Safe Around Strangers

Lesson Focus
Be safe around strangers.

Vocabulary
stranger
danger

A **stranger** is someone you do not know. A stranger can put you in danger. You are in **danger** when you are not safe.

Stay away from strangers. Do not go anywhere with them. Never tell strangers your name or where you live. Do not open the door to strangers at home.

1. Say NO!

2. Get away.

3. Tell someone.

Take these three steps if a stranger bothers you. Say NO. Get away. Then tell someone.

You do not have to be nice if a stranger tries to talk to you. You can yell. You can run away.

Always tell an adult you trust about strangers.

Review

1. **Vocabulary** What is a **stranger**?

2. How can you be safe around strangers?

3. 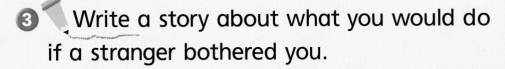 Write a story about what you would do if a stranger bothered you.

LIFE SKILLS

Communicate

Know how to get help if you are lost. You need to communicate with the right people. You **communicate** when you talk to others.

1 **Decide whom to talk to.**

Nick is lost in a store. He wants to get help. He looks for a police officer, a guard, or a store clerk.

2 **Say what you need to say.**

I am lost. I need to find my mom.

Nick sees a store clerk. Nick tells the clerk he needs help. He says he is lost.

3 Listen carefully. Answer any questions.

Where did you last see your mom?

The clerk asks questions to find out more about Nick's mother. Nick answers him clearly.

4 Follow directions.

I will call for your mom.

Nick follows the clerk. The clerk calls for Nick's mother. He uses the store's loudspeaker.

 Problem Solving

Use the steps to solve this problem.

You and an older family member are in a crowded mall. You stop to tie your shoe. You can not see your family member when you look up. How should you get help?

Avoiding Poisons

A **poison** is something that can make you sick if you swallow it or breathe it. Some poisons can even kill you.

Some things in your home may have poisons in them. They should be kept in a safe place.

Know the signs and pictures that mark poisons. Do not touch things that have these signs.

Many cleaning products and insect sprays have poisons in them. Only adults can use them safely. Never use them on your own.

Review

1 **Vocabulary** What is a **poison**?

2 Why should poisons be kept in a safe place?

3 Write a warning. Tell others to stay away from poisons.

Avoiding Weapons

Lesson Focus
Stay away
from
weapons.

Vocabulary
weapons

Weapons are things that can be used to hurt others. Guns and knives are weapons.

Tell a trusted adult if you see a weapon. You can tell a parent or an older family member. You can tell a police officer. You can tell a teacher if you see a gun in or near school.

Stay away from weapons. Never touch them. Weapons are not toys. They can hurt you and others.

Review

1 **Vocabulary** What is a **weapon**?

2 What should you do if you see a weapon?

3 Write a play. Tell what two friends could do if they saw a weapon near school.

Math

Safe Places Graph

How many children chose their grandmother's house?

How many children chose their backyard?

Make your own graph about safe places.

Safe Places We Like

my backyard						
grandmother's house						
friend's house						

0 1 2 3 4 5 6

Writing

Safety Rules for School

Make a poster. Write five or more school safety rules. Hang your poster in a school hallway.

My Rules for a Safe School

1. Tell a teacher if you see a stranger.

2.

GO ONLINE **For more activities, visit The Learning Site.**
www.harcourtschool.com/health

Citizenship

Keeping Your School Safe

You can make your school a safe place in which to learn. Look out for things that can hurt others. Tell a trusted adult if you see weapons or poisons. Point out strangers.

A **citizen** is a person who belongs to a community. You are a good citizen when you help keep your school safe.

How is this child being a good citizen?

Activity

What would you do if a stranger bothers you at school? Work with a partner. Act out what you would do.

ALL VISITORS MUST CHECK IN

Use Health Words

Use the word to tell about the picture.

1 stranger

2 danger

3 poison

4 weapon

Focus Skill Reading Skill

5 Recall and retell what you learned about staying away from poisons.

Recall Detail	Retell
Recall Detail	
Recall Detail	

Use Life Skills

Look at the picture. Then
answer the questions.

6 Who should you tell if you get
lost in a store?

7 What are four steps you can
use to communicate?

Write About It

8 Make a list of the three
things you should do if a
stranger bothers you.

8 Staying Well

Find Cause and Effect

An effect is something that happens. A cause is the reason something happens.

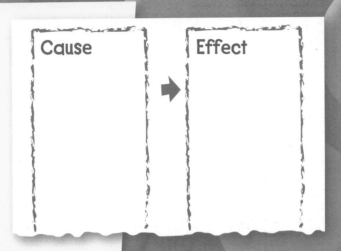

Cause		Effect

Health Graph

Our Illnesses This Year

6
5
4
3
2
1
0

flu   cold   other illnesses

Daily Physical Activity

You should exercise every day to help your body stay well.

 **Be Active!**
Use **Jumping and Pumping** on Track 8.

Sometimes You Are Ill

Lesson Focus
You are ill
when you are
not feeling
well.

Vocabulary
ill

People of all ages become ill sometimes. If you are **ill**, you are sick. You do not feel well when you are ill. Parts of your body may hurt. You may feel very tired.

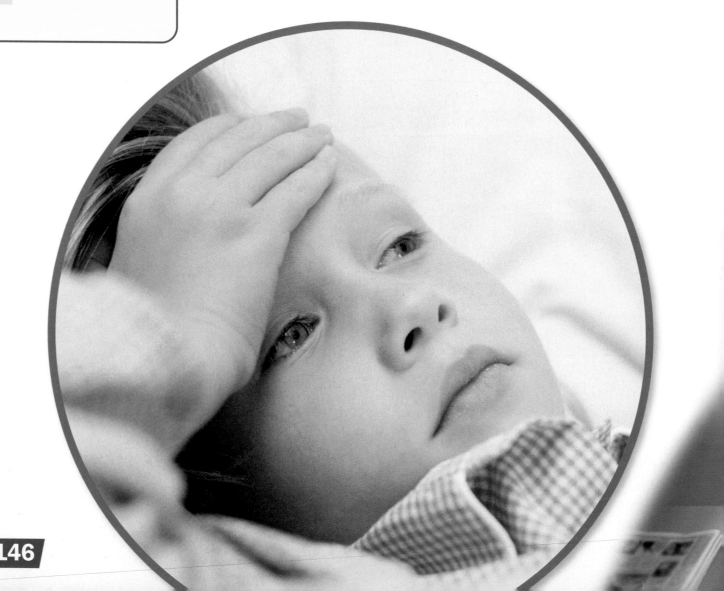

Tell your teacher if you feel ill at school. Tell your family if you feel ill at home. Show or tell what hurts.

Your parents may take you to visit a doctor when you are ill. Tell the doctor how you feel.

You may get a cold. Your nose may run. You may have watery eyes. You may sneeze and cough. You may have a sore throat.

You may get the flu. Some signs of the flu are like the signs of a cold. You may also have a fever that makes your skin feel hot. Your body may hurt all over.

Review

1 **Vocabulary** What happens when you are **ill**?

2 What should you do if you feel ill?

3 Write a story about a boy or girl who is ill. Tell how he or she feels.

Communicate

You **communicate** when you talk to someone. It is important to communicate when you do not feel well.

1 **Decide whom to talk to.**

Rob is not feeling well in class. He wants to tell his teacher.

2 **Say what you need to say.**

I think I am sick. My stomach hurts.

Rob raises his hand. He tells his teacher how he feels.

3 Listen carefully.
Answer any questions.

4 Get information.

Are you hurting in other places?

No. Just my stomach hurts.

The teacher asks Rob questions about his pain. Rob answers the questions clearly.

Lie down here and rest for a while.

The teacher sends Rob to talk with the school nurse. The nurse tells Rob what to do to feel better.

 Problem Solving

Use the steps to solve this problem.

You are at home with your family. You feel pain in your ear. Whom should you tell? What should you say about how you feel?

Preventing Illness

Germs can cause disease. If you have a **disease**, you are ill.

Disease spreads when people spread germs. You can spread germs when you cough, sneeze, or blow your nose.

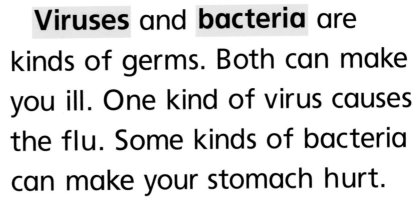

Viruses and **bacteria** are kinds of germs. Both can make you ill. One kind of virus causes the flu. Some kinds of bacteria can make your stomach hurt.

How are these children spreading germs?

Vaccines are medicines that keep your body from getting some diseases. Most children start getting vaccines when they are babies. Vaccines can help you stay well.

You can help stop germs from spreading. Cover your nose and mouth when you sneeze or cough. Wash your hands often. Never touch your eyes, nose, or mouth with unwashed hands.

Review

1. **Vocabulary** What does a **vaccine** do?

2. How do people spread germs?

3. Write about how to stop spreading germs at school.

Allergies

Lesson Focus
An allergy is
an unhealthy
way your
body reacts to
something
around you.

Vocabulary
allergy

An **allergy** is an unhealthy way your body reacts to something around you. An allergy is not a disease.

Allergies can make your eyes and nose itch. They can make you sneeze or give you a rash. Allergies can also make it hard for you to breathe.

Different people have allergies to different things. Some people have many allergies. Others have none.

If you have allergies, a doctor can help you feel better. Stay away from things that bother your allergies.

Review

1 **Vocabulary** What is an **allergy**?

2 What can allergies do?

3 Write about what you can do if you have an allergy.

Staying Well

You can do many things to help yourself stay well.

Lesson Focus
You can do many things to stay well.

Stay clean.

Eat healthful foods.

Get checkups.

Get enough sleep.

Exercise.

Review

1 What can you do to stay well?

2 How does exercise help you stay well?

3 Write what you did yesterday to stay well.

ACTIVITIES

Math

Hand-Washings Graph

How many washings took place on Monday?

How many more washings took place on Friday than on Tuesday?

Make a graph about staying clean.

Times I Washed My Hands at School

Monday	🤚	🤚	🤚	🤚	
Tuesday	🤚	🤚	🤚		
Wednesday	🤚	🤚	🤚		
Thursday	🤚	🤚	🤚	🤚	
Friday	🤚	🤚	🤚	🤚	🤚

Writing

Make a Book

Draw pictures of some things you do to stay well. Write a sentence for each picture. Make your pictures into a book. Share it with others.

I run often!

 For more activities, visit The Learning Site.
www.harcourtschool.com/health

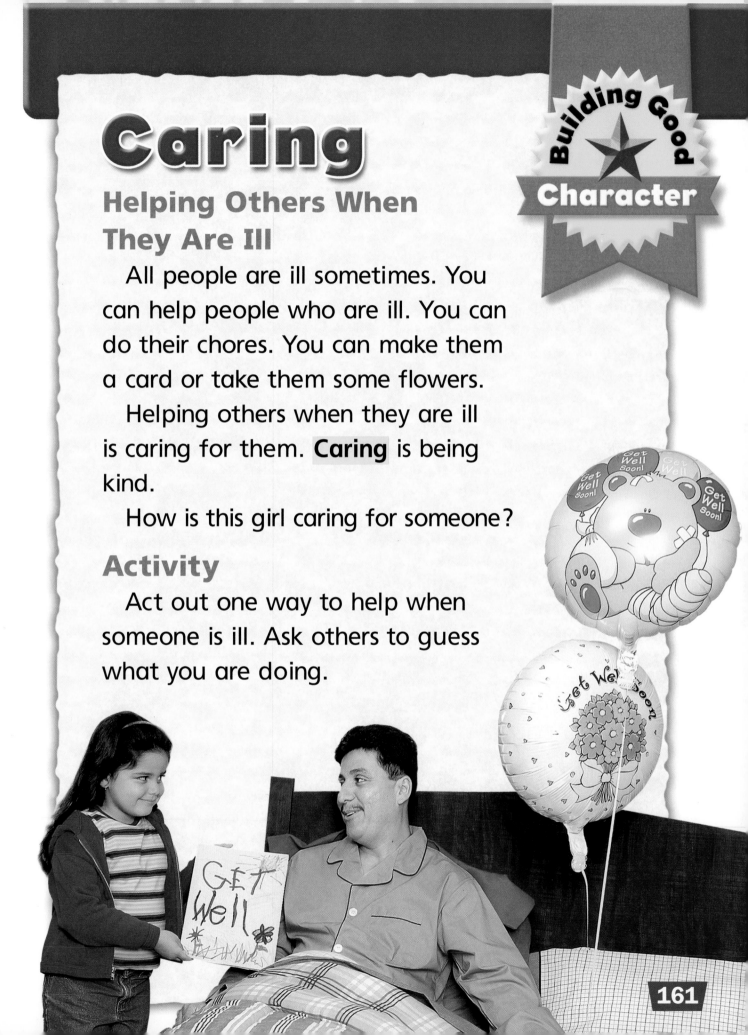

Caring

Helping Others When They Are Ill

All people are ill sometimes. You can help people who are ill. You can do their chores. You can make them a card or take them some flowers.

Helping others when they are ill is caring for them. **Caring** is being kind.

How is this girl caring for someone?

Activity

Act out one way to help when someone is ill. Ask others to guess what you are doing.

Use Health Words

Use each word to tell about the picture.

1 allergy

2 ill

3 bacteria

4 vaccines

Focus Skill Reading Skill

5 Tell two causes for the effect.

Cause		Effect
	→	I do not spread germs.

Use Life Skills

Look at the pictures. Then answer the questions.

6 Which picture shows how Rob communicates?

7 What are four steps you can use to communicate when you feel ill?

Write About It

8 Write about a sign that shows you may be ill. Why should you tell someone when you feel ill?

You cough a lot. You should tell someone so you can get help.

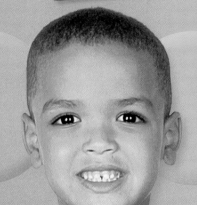

CHAPTER 9

About Medicines and Drugs

Say No to Drugs

Reading Skill

Find the Main Idea

The main idea of something you are reading is what it is mostly about. The details tell more about it.

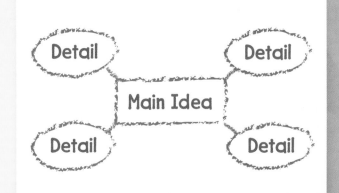

Health Graph

Say NO Signs	
Sunday	⊘ ⊘ ⊘
Monday	⊘ ⊘ ⊘ ⊘
Tuesday	⊘ ⊘
Wednesday	⊘ ⊘ ⊘
Thursday	⊘ ⊘ ⊘
Friday	⊘ ⊘ ⊘ ⊘
Saturday	⊘

Key: Each ⊘ stands for 2 signs.

Daily Physical Activity

Say NO to drugs and exercise every day. Keep your body healthy.

 **Be Active!** Use **Hop to It** on Track 9.

Using Medicines Safely

Medicines can help you feel better. Some medicines help you get well when you are ill. Others keep you from getting ill. Some medicines are pills. Some are liquids, powders, or creams.

Some medicines can look or taste like candy. But medicines are NOT candy. They can harm you.

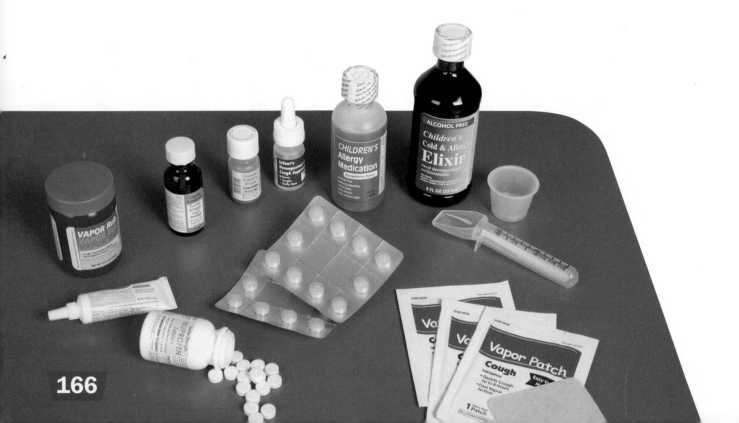

Medicines should be kept in a safe place. Only adult family members, doctors, or nurses should give you medicines. Do not touch or take them on your own.

Medicines are drugs. **Drugs** change the way your body works.

You need a special note from a doctor to buy some medicines. Other medicines are sold on the shelves in stores. Adults can buy them without a note from a doctor.

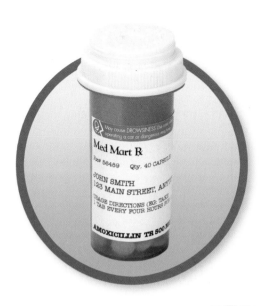

All medicines have labels. Your parents should read the labels. Labels tell you what medicines do. They also tell you how to take medicines.

Review

① **Vocabulary** What are **medicines**?

② Who should give you medicines?

③ Write a label for a medicine. Tell what it does and how to take it.

Drugs

Some drugs are not medicines. They do not help you. They can harm your body.

Some drugs are legal. **Legal** means that the law allows people to take them. Some are legal for everyone. Some are legal only for adults.

Caffeine is a drug. It is legal for all people. It is in some soft drinks. It is also in chocolate and some teas and coffees.

Caffeine can change how your body works. It makes your heart beat fast. It can keep you awake at night. Too much caffeine is not good for you.

Which of these foods and drinks have caffeine?

Review

1 **Vocabulary** What does **legal** mean?

2 What can caffeine do to you?

3 Write a list of some drinks that do not have caffeine.

Tobacco and the Body

Lesson Focus
Tobacco has drugs in it that can harm your body.

Vocabulary
tobacco
habit
tobacco smoke

There are drugs in tobacco. **Tobacco** is in cigarettes and cigars. Some adults smoke it in pipes. Some chew it. Tobacco is not legal for children.

A **habit** is something people do over and over. Using tobacco is a habit that harms people's health. This habit is hard to stop.

FULL FLAVOR

CIGARETTES

20 CLASS A CIGARETTES

The drugs in tobacco make the heart beat fast. They cause lung disease and cancer.

Other people's tobacco smoke can harm your lungs and heart. Smoke from tobacco is **tobacco smoke**. Stay away from tobacco and tobacco smoke.

Review

1. **Vocabulary** What is a **habit**?

2. How can tobacco harm you?

3. Write two or more reasons people should not use tobacco.

Alcohol and the Body

Lesson Focus
Alcohol is a drug that is bad for your body.

Vocabulary
alcohol

Alcohol is a drug. It is in beer and wine. It is also in some other drinks.

Alcohol can harm people. It changes the way the brain works. It slows down thinking. This can cause accidents.

Drinking too much alcohol can make a person sick.

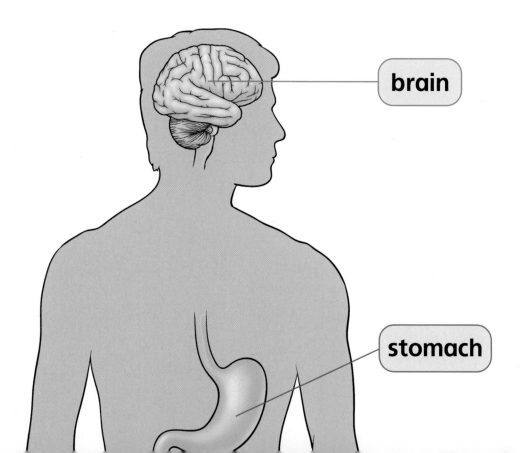

brain

stomach

Drinking alcohol is not legal for children. Stay away from alcohol.

Review

1 **Vocabulary** What is **alcohol**?

2 How can alcohol harm people?

3 Write a list of some drinks that do not have alcohol in them.

Staying Away from Drugs

You can refuse drugs. To **refuse** is to say NO. Refuse to take medicines that are not yours. Take medicines only from adult family members, doctors, or nurses.

Say NO to alcohol and tobacco. Tell an adult right away if you see drugs.

Many ads make using alcohol or tobacco look like fun. These ads do not tell how drugs can harm you.

Listen to your parents, teacher, and doctor. Think about how drugs can harm you. Say NO to drugs.

Review

1. **Vocabulary** What does **refuse** mean?

2. Why should you say NO to drugs?

3. Write two or more ways you can say NO to drugs.

Say NO to Drugs

Get help from trusted adults when you feel ill. They will help you use medicines safely. Say NO to using medicines that are not yours. Here is how.

1 **Say NO. Tell why not.**

No, thanks. Your medicine might not be good for me.

Liz has a sore throat. Jay wants to give Liz his medicine. Liz says NO.

2 **Think about what could happen.**

Liz knows that Jay's medicine could harm her. It could make her feel worse.

3 Suggest something else to do.

Let's play a game.

Liz thinks her throat might feel better if she stops thinking about it.

4 Go home if you need to.

I will call my mom for help.

Liz still feels ill. She calls her mother to come and take her home.

Problem Solving

Use the steps to solve this problem.

You and your friend find a bottle of pills. Your friend says the pills look like candy. She wants you to try some. What should you do?

ACTIVITIES

Math

Caffeine-Free Drinks Graph

How many children chose water?

How many children chose juice?

Make your own graph about caffeine-free drinks.

Writing

Make a Promise

Write a promise to say NO to drugs. Explain how your promise will help you stay healthy. Then sign it.

 For more activities, visit The Learning Site.
www.harcourtschool.com/health

Respect

Respecting Yourself

You should respect yourself just as you respect others. You can do this by taking good care of yourself.

You know what is good and bad for your health. You say NO to drugs that can harm you. You don't let people push you to make bad choices.

How are the people in this family showing respect for themselves?

Activity

Draw a picture that shows one way you respect yourself. Write a sentence about it.

Use Health Words

Tell which picture goes best with the word.

1. **medicines**

2. **caffeine**

3. **tobacco**

4. **alcohol**

a.

b.

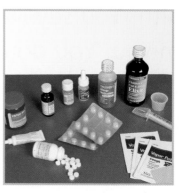

c.

d.

Reading Skill

5. Tell the main idea.

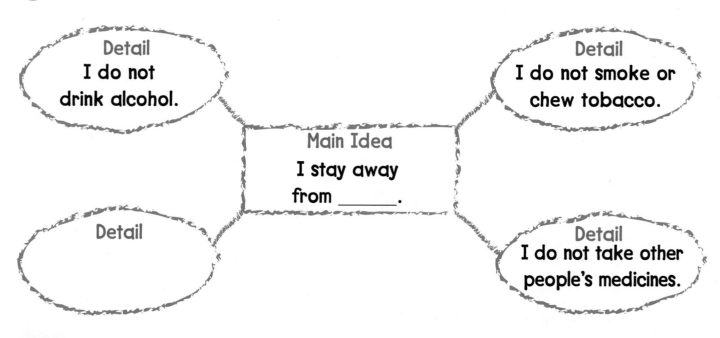

Detail
I do not drink alcohol.

Detail
I do not smoke or chew tobacco.

Main Idea
I stay away from _____.

Detail

Detail
I do not take other people's medicines.

Use Life Skills

Look at the picture. Then answer the questions.

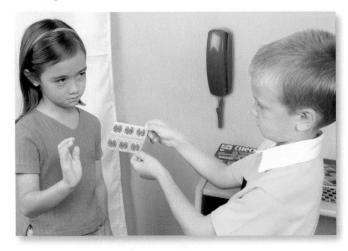

6 What is the right thing to do if you feel ill away from home?

7 What are four steps you can use to say NO to medicines that are not yours?

Write About It

8 Make a list of three drugs. Write about why you stay away from each one.

1. tobacco

I do not use tobacco. It can harm me.

CHAPTER 10

You Have Feelings

Reading Skill

Focus Skill

Use Context Clues

The words, pictures, and charts near a new word can help you read and understand it.

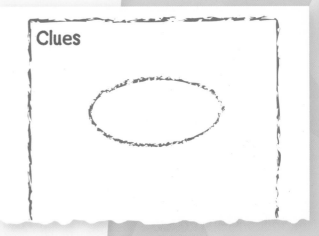

Clues

Health Graph

What Makes Us Happy

pets

grandparents

friends

0 1 2 3 4 5

Daily Physical Activity

Exercise can help you feel better when you are angry. Exercise every day.

Be Active!
Use **Super Stress Buster** on Track 10.

You Are Special

Lesson Focus
All people are special.

Vocabulary
special

All people are special. **Special** means different from all others. No one looks or acts just like you. These things make you special.

People like to do different things. You can do some things very well. That makes you special, too.

How are these children special?

Review

1 Vocabulary What does **special** mean?

2 What can you do well?

3 Write a list of things that make you special.

Showing Your Feelings

Lesson Focus
Everyone has feelings.

Vocabulary
feelings
angry

Everyone has feelings. **Feelings** are what you feel when you are happy, sad, afraid, or excited.

Sometimes you like the way you feel. Sometimes you do not.

How do these children feel?

Everyone feels angry sometimes. **Angry** means mad. It is OK to feel angry. It is not OK to hurt people when you are angry.

Talking can help you feel better when you are angry. So can exercise and play.

You can use words to tell how you feel. It is good to talk about your feelings with your family and friends.

You can show how you feel. You may smile when you are happy. You may cry when you are sad.

Show your feelings in ways that will not hurt others. Think about how others may feel.

How are these children showing their feelings?

Review

1. **Vocabulary** What are some **feelings**?

2. How can you show how you feel?

3. Write a poem. Tell about things that make you feel happy.

LIFE SKILLS

Manage Stress

Doing something new can cause stress. You feel **stress** when you are worried or excited. These steps show how to manage stress.

1 **Know what stress feels like.**

Nan will be sleeping at a friend's house for the first time. She feels stress. It gives her a stomachache.

2 **Figure out what is making you feel stress.**

Nan is worried about being in a different house. She might not be able to go to sleep.

3 Do something that will help you feel better. Talk to someone you trust.

4 Think about doing well instead of feeling stress.

Nan talks to her mother about her stress. Her mother tells her to think of the fun she will have.

Nan thinks about having fun at her friend's house. This helps her feel better.

 Problem Solving

Use the steps to solve this problem.

Your class is going on a big field trip. You will go on a long bus ride for the first time. You feel stress. How can you manage your stress?

You Are a Friend

Lesson Focus
Good friends are kind to one another.

Vocabulary
friend

A **friend** is a person you know and like. Good friends are kind. They share and help. Friends talk and listen to one another. They play together. Friends are fun!

You can make new friends. You can talk to or play with friends.

There are good ways to act to get attention from friends. How are these children being good friends?

Review

1 **Vocabulary** What is a **friend**?

2 What can friends do together?

3 Write a story about good friends.

Respecting Others

Lesson Focus
Showing respect and being polite help you get along with others.

Vocabulary
respect
good touch
polite

You **respect** others when you treat them nicely. This helps you get along better.

Do not talk when others are talking. Show respect in school by raising your hand before you speak.

You have needs and wants. Needs are things you must have to live. Wants are things you would like to have but do not need.

Show respect when you ask for things you need or want. Speak nicely. Do not yell.

People can also show respect in the way they touch others. A **good touch** can be a hug or a pat on the back. A bad touch can make you feel uncomfortable. If someone touches you in a bad way, say NO. Then tell a trusted adult right away.

Being **polite** is a way to show you care about others. Knocking before you go into a room is one way to be polite. Being helpful is also polite.

Be polite when you talk. Say please when you ask for things. Say thank you when someone helps you.

Review

1. **Vocabulary** What does **respect** mean?

2. How can you be polite?

3. Write about two ways you can show respect.

ACTIVITIES

Math

Friends Graph

How many children said they ride bikes?

How many children said they read?

Make your own graph about friends.

Things We Do with Friends

read	☺	☺	☺		
ride bikes	☺	☺	☺	☺	☺
play games	☺	☺			

Key: Each ☺ equals 2 children.

Writing

A Friendly Letter

Write a letter to a friend. Tell what makes him or her a good friend. Then give your friend the letter.

Dear Jane,
I think you are a great friend because you are kind to me.
Your friend,

Lisa

For more activities, visit The Learning Site.
www.harcourtschool.com/health

Caring

Building Good **Character**

Being a Good Friend

You can show you **care** by being a good friend. Be polite and kind. Share snacks, toys, and other things.

Be honest with your friends. Then they can trust you. Help them when they need help. Then they may help you.

How is this girl being a good friend?

Activity

Work with a partner. Act out ways you can be a good friend.

Chapter Review

Use Health Words

Use each word to tell about the picture.

1 polite

2 angry

3 friend

4 respect

(Focus Skill) Reading Skill

5 Read the clues in the box. Use them to figure out the word that belongs in the center.

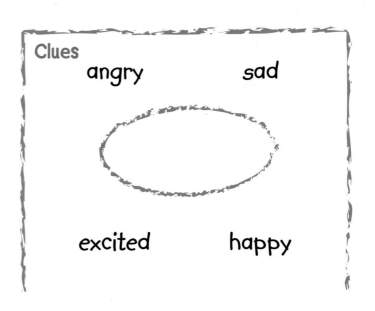

Clues

angry   sad

excited   happy

Use Life Skills

Look at the picture. Then answer the question.

6 Who should you talk to when you feel stress?

7 What are four steps you can use to manage stress?

Write About It

8 Draw a picture of someone you know. Write about what makes that person special.

My uncle is special because he is a good cook.

Your Family

Recall and Retell

To recall is to remember what you have read. To retell is to tell it in your own words.

Recall Detail	Retell
Recall Detail	
Recall Detail	

Health Graph

Favorite Places to Visit with Family

park	❤ ❤ ❤
beach	❤ ❤ ❤ ❤
museum	❤ ❤

Key: Each ❤ stands for 5 children.

Daily Physical Activity

You should exercise every day. The people in your family can exercise together.

 **Be Active!**
Use **Funky Flex** on Track 11.

Families

You have a family. Each family is different. Each family is special. People in a family love and care for one another. **Love** is a special feeling of caring.

You can show you love and care for people in your family. You can talk and eat with them. You can play games and read with them. You can exercise with them, too.

Review

1 **Vocabulary** What is **love**?

2 What is something you can do with your family?

3 Write a list. Tell ways you can show people in your family that you care for them.

Families Change

Your family can change. If a new baby comes, the family will get bigger. If someone moves away, the family will get smaller.

Changes can make you feel different ways. Some changes may make you happy. Some may make you sad. You can tell a parent or another family member how you feel.

Review

1 How might you feel about family changes?

2 Whom can you tell about your feelings?

3 Write a story about a family that changes.

Families Work Together

Lesson Focus

People in a family work together in many ways.

People in a family work together to stay healthy and happy. They help one another. They share the work. They are kind and polite.

How are the people in this family working together?

People in a family work together to get things done. Each person has jobs to do at home. Working together helps family members get along.

People in a family help one another feel good. Your family can help you when you are hurt or sad. Your family can also help you solve problems.

Review

❶ How can people in a family work together?

❷ How can your family help you?

❸ Write one way to help your family for each day of the week. Make a chart.

Resolve Conflicts

People in families sometimes have conflicts. They can work together to resolve them. These steps show how.

1 **Agree that there is a problem.**

I need more blocks.

Luis does not have many blocks. His sister Nina has a lot. Nina will not share them.

2 **Listen to each other.**

Luis tells Nina why he needs some of her blocks. Luis wants to make a building. Nina listens to Luis.

3 **Think of ways to work together.**

Luis and Nina have an idea. They can make something together.

4 **Find a way for both sides to win.**

Luis and Nina have fun working on one big castle. It looks great!

Problem Solving

Use the steps to solve this problem.

You and your brother have a new board game. Your brother wants to play it with his friend. You want to play it with your friend. How could you resolve this conflict?

ACTIVITIES

Math

Helping Graph

How many times did Ann put away her toys?

How many times did she help in all?

Make your own graph about helping.

How Ann Helped This Week

0 1 2 3 4 5 6 7

Writing

Thank-You Card

Who in your family has done something nice for you? Write a list of people. Choose one person. Say thank you by making a special card for him or her.

Thank You, Mom

 GO ONLINE For more activities, visit The Learning Site.
www.harcourtschool.com/health

Fairness

Being Fair with Your Family and Friends

Be fair when you work or play with others. You will often need to share supplies, toys, and games. Do not take more than anyone else. Take turns if you need to. Be sure that there is a way for everyone to play.

How are these children being fair?

Activity

Write a story about how you share with your family and friends. Tell ways you are fair.

Chapter Review

Use Health Words

1 Tell how the family in this picture is showing **love** .

Reading Skill

Recall what you learned about families.

2 Recall Detail	**Retell** People in a family work together.
3 Recall Detail	
4 Recall Detail	

Use Life Skills

Look at the pictures. Then answer the questions.

5 Which picture shows a conflict?

6 How do the children resolve their conflict?

7 What are four steps you can use to resolve conflicts?

Write About It

8 Write a list of things that people in a family can do together.

People in a family can eat together.

CHAPTER 12

A Healthful Neighborhood

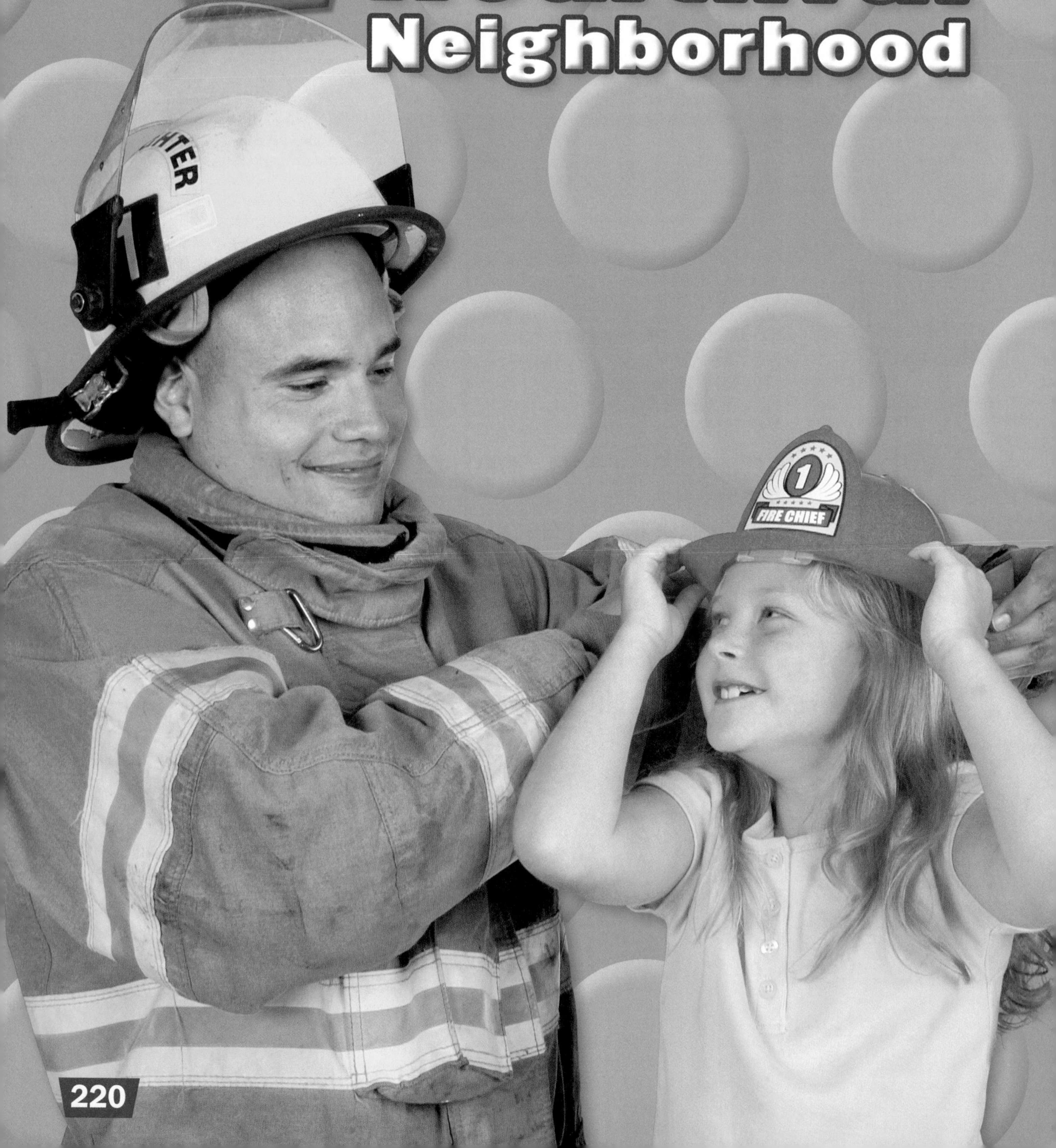

Make Predictions

When you make a prediction, you tell what you think will happen next.

> **Prediction**
>
> **What Happened**

Health Graph

Community Helpers I Saw This Week

police officer	
firefighter	
nurse	

0 1 2 3 4 5 6

Daily Physical Activity

You should exercise every day. Find places in your community where you can exercise safely.

Be Active!
Use **Broadway Bound** on Track 12.

Community Helpers

Lesson Focus
People in your community help you stay safe and healthy.

Vocabulary
community
nurse
clinic
doctor

A **community** is a place where people live and work. Each community has workers who help keep people safe and healthy.

Police officers help keep you safe. Firefighters put out fires. Other workers help you when you are hurt or ill.

Look at the pictures. How do these workers help the community?

A **nurse** helps you when you are hurt or ill. A nurse also helps you stay healthy. Some nurses work in clinics. A **clinic** is a place where you can get help if you are ill.

You might see a school nurse if you are hurt or ill or if you need health information. The nurse may also check your eyes and ears. You should cooperate with the school nurse.

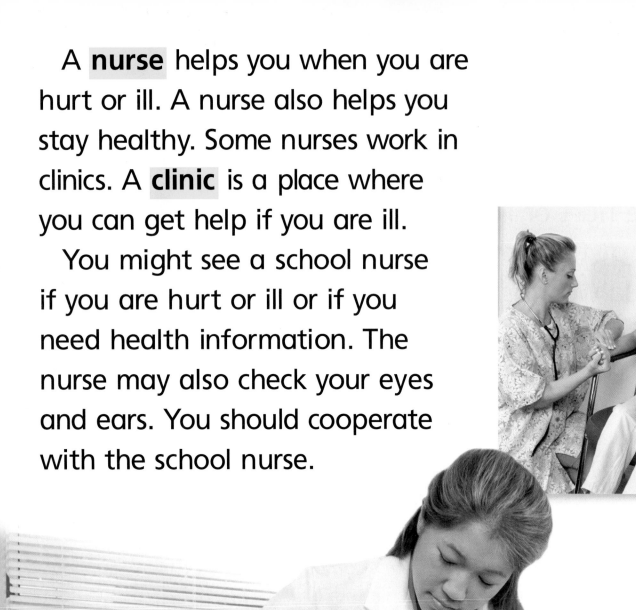

A **doctor** also helps you when you are hurt or ill. Doctors can find out why you are ill. They can help you feel better.

Some doctors take care of your whole body. Others take care of just one part.

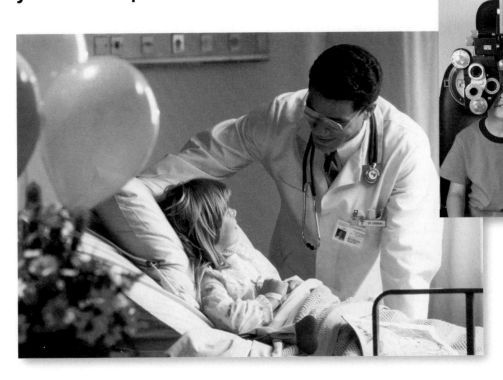

Review

1 **Vocabulary** What is a **community**?

2 Which community workers could help you if you were ill?

3 Write a list of community workers. Tell how each one helps you.

225

Pollution

Lesson Focus

A healthful environment is clean and safe.

Vocabulary

environment

pollution

litter

The **environment** is the land, water, and air around you. A healthful environment is clean and safe.

Pollution is waste that harms the environment. It can make people unhealthy. We all need clean land, air, and water.

FARM FRESH

Where do you see
pollution in this picture?

Litter is trash that is not put in the right place. Having trash all around is not healthful. Trash has germs that can make you ill.

Put trash in its place. Never throw it onto the ground.

EXIT

Some workers help keep your community clean and safe. They pick up trash.

How are all these people keeping the environment clean?

Review

1 **Vocabulary** What is **litter**?

2 Why is pollution harmful?

3 Write about two ways you can help keep the environment clean.

Make Decisions

How should you get rid of things after you use them? Keep your community clean by making the right decision. Here is how.

1 **Think about the choices.**

Mike looks at his empty juice box. He could throw it onto the ground. He could put it in a trash can.

2 **Say NO to choices that are against the law or your family's rules.**

PLEASE DO NOT LITTER

Mike reads the sign. He knows that it is against the law to litter.

3 Ask yourself what could happen with each choice.

Litter will make the park dirty. Putting trash in a trash can will keep the park clean.

4 Make the best choice.

PLEASE DO NOT LITTER

Mike decides to throw his juice box into the trash can. His choice helps keep the park clean.

Problem Solving

Use the steps to solve this problem.

You have finished eating lunch. What should you do with your paper cup and plate?

Recycling

You can make less trash if you recycle things. To **recycle** is to turn used things into new things. You can recycle paper, cans, and bottles.

Wheat Squares

Wheat Squares
100% Natural Whole Grain Wheat Cereal

WE RECYCLE

Many new things can be made from used paper, cans, and bottles. Look at the pictures. What new things can be made?

Review

1 **Vocabulary** What happens when you **recycle**?

2 What can you recycle?

3 Write a plan. Tell how you can make less trash.

Math

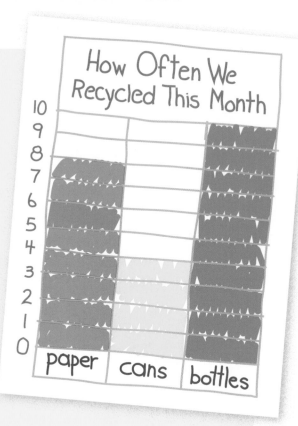

How Often We Recycled This Month

Recycling Graph

What was recycled most often?

What was recycled least often?

Make a graph about recycling.

You Are Invited to Our Community Helper Day

Writing

Invite a Helper

Make a card that asks a community helper to speak at your school. Write what you want to learn from the helper. Then send your card.

Citizenship

Building Good Character

Taking Pride in Your School

Citizenship is taking pride in your community. You can show good citizenship at school.

Follow school rules. They help keep everyone safe. Keep your school clean. That will help make it a healthful place to learn in.

How are these children being good citizens?

Activity

Write about how you show good citizenship at school.

Use Health Words

Use each word
to tell about
the picture.

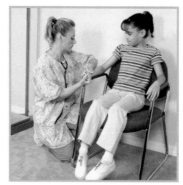

1 nurse

2 clinic

3 environment

4 pollution

 **Reading Skill**

5 Predict what will
happen if people
do not litter. Look at
page 231 for clues.

Prediction

What Happened

Use Life Skills

Look at the pictures. Then answer the questions.

6 Which picture shows trash that has been put in the right place?

7 What are four steps you can use to make decisions about where to put your trash?

Write About It

8 Write about three places in your community. Name the kinds of community workers who work at each one.

Firefighters work at a fire station.

Find Cause and Effect

Learning how to find cause and effect can help you understand what you read. You can use a chart like this to help you find cause and effect.

Cause		Effect
A cause is why something happens.		An effect is what happens.

Some paragraphs have more than one cause or effect. Read this paragraph.

> Judy runs every day. This helps keep her heart strong. It also helps her fight off germs. Exercise is good for her body.

This chart shows a cause and its effects in the paragraph.

Cause		Effect
Judy runs every day.		Judy's heart is strong. Judy can fight off germs.

Find the Main Idea

Learning how to find the main idea can help you understand what you read. The main idea of a paragraph is what it is mostly about. The details tell more about it.

Read this paragraph.

> Never take medicines by yourself. Angie tells her mom that she feels ill. Her mom gets medicine from a high cabinet. Angie can not reach it. Medicine must be kept in a safe place.

This chart shows the main idea and details.

Detail
Angie feels ill.

Detail
Angie can not reach the medicine.

Main Idea
Never take medicines by yourself.

Detail
Angie's mom gets her medicine.

Detail
Medicines must be kept in a safe place.

Make Predictions

Learning how to make predictions can help you understand what you read. A prediction is what you think will happen next.

Some paragraphs give clues to help you predict what will happen next.

Edie wants to ride a bike that is too big for her. Edie's mom tells her she will be big enough to ride the bike next year. Edie walks over to her own bike.

This chart shows the prediction made from a clue in the paragraph.

Prediction

I think Edie will ride her own bike.

What Happened

Edie walks over to her own bike.

Recall and Retell

Focus Skill

Learning how to recall and retell details can help you understand what you read. Some sentences tell the main idea. Some sentences tell details.

Read this paragraph.

> Tim was playing on the climbing bars. He hurt his leg when he jumped off. Next time Tim will not jump from the bars.

This chart shows how to recall and retell what the paragraph is about.

	Retell
Recall Detail Tim was playing on the climbing bars.	Tim jumped off the climbing bars. He got hurt.
Recall Detail Tim jumped off the bars.	
Recall Detail Tim hurt his leg.	

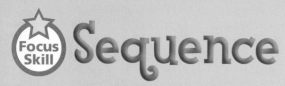 **Sequence**

Learning how to find sequence can help you understand what you read. You can use a chart like this to help you find sequence.

1 The first step.	→	2 The next step.	→	3 The last step.

Some paragraphs use words that help you understand order. Read this paragraph. Look at the underlined words.

> Brush your teeth every day. <u>First</u>, brush the outsides. <u>Next</u>, brush the insides. <u>Last</u>, brush the flat parts of your back teeth. Brushing helps keep your teeth clean and healthy.

This chart shows the sequence of the paragraph.

1 Brush the outsides.	→	2 Brush the insides.	→	3 Brush the flat parts of your back teeth.

Focus Skill

Use Context Clues

Learning how to use context clues can help you understand what you read. Context clues are words or pictures near a word. You can use a chart to help you use context clues.

Some paragraphs use words that may be new to you. Read this paragraph. Look for clues to find the meaning of the underlined word.

Steve shows his <u>feelings</u> in different ways. He uses words to show he is angry. He laughs when he is happy. He cries when he is sad. He jumps high when he is excited.

This chart shows the context clues in the paragraph.

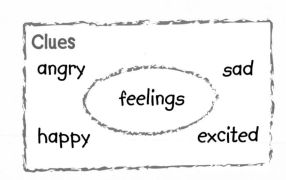

Clues
angry   sad
          feelings
happy   excited

Health and Safety

First Aid for Kids

You can help someone who is hurt and stay safe, too. You will need to know these things.

Know when to call 911.

Know how the body works.

Know how to check for safety.

Know how to prevent injury.

Earthquake Safety Tips

- If you are outside, stay there. Move away from buildings and electric wires.

- If you are inside, go under a doorway or a heavy table or desk. Stay away from glass doors and windows.

- After the earthquake there may be aftershocks. Watch for falling objects.

Storm Safety Tips

In a Tornado

Go to a safe area away from doors and windows. A hallway or basement is best.

In a Hurricane

Stay in a room in the middle of the house. Listen to weather reports for what to do.

Stranger Danger

Be safe. Follow these rules.

- Never talk to strangers.

- Never go anywhere with a stranger.

- Do not open the door if you are home alone.

- Do not tell anyone on the telephone that you are home alone unless you are calling 911.

- Do not give your name, address, or telephone number to a stranger.

- If you are lost, tell a police officer, a guard, or a store clerk.

Prevent Poisoning

A poison is something that can kill you or make you very ill. Some poisons have special uses. Only adults can use them safely.

These pictures mark a poison.

Keep Away from Poisons

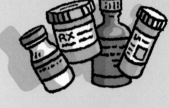

- Know the pictures and words that mark poisons.

- Never take any medicines or vitamins by yourself. Always ask an adult to help you.

- Never use cleaning products by yourself. Never mix cleaning products.

- Never use insect sprays or lotions by yourself. Always ask an adult to help you.

My Internet Safety Rules

1 I will never give anyone my name or address unless my parents know about it.

2 I will tell my parents if I see something that does not seem right for me to see.

3 I will never agree to get together with someone I meet online.

4 I will talk with my parents about rules for going online. I will follow those rules.

Family Emergency Plan

Your family can be safe in an emergency by following a plan.

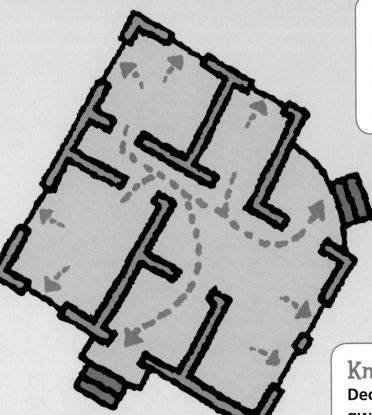

Have Two Meeting Places
Decide on two places to meet. One should be about a block away and the other at least a mile away.

Know What Could Happen
Learn what emergencies might happen in your area.

Know Your Family Contact
Decide on someone who lives far away to be a contact person. Know the person's name, address, and telephone number.

Have Emergency Drills
Practice getting out of your home safely.

Make an Emergency Kit
Gather first-aid items, food, and water.

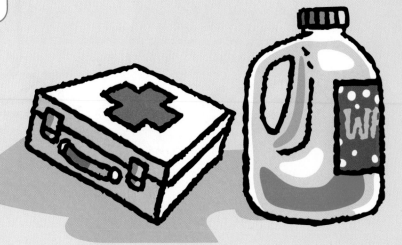

Backpack Safety

Carrying a backpack that is too heavy can injure your back. Carrying one the wrong way can also hurt you.

Right way   **Wrong way**

Glossary

ad (AD): a message that tries to get you to buy a product (32)

alcohol (AL•kuh•hawl): the drug found in beer, wine, and liquor (174)

allergy (AL•er•jee): an unhealthy way your body reacts to something around you (156)

angry (ANG•gree): feeling upset with someone or about something (189)

bacteria (bak•TIR•ee•uh): a kind of germ (153)

blood vessels (BLUHD VEH•suhlz): tubes that carry blood through your body (16)

breakfast (BREK•fuhst): the meal most people eat in the morning (70)

caffeine (ka•FEEN): the legal drug found in coffee, tea, chocolate, and some soft drinks (170)

care (KAIR): to be kind and helpful (201)

caring (KAIR•ing): being kind and helpful (161)

citizen (SIH•tuh•zuhn): a person who belongs to a community (141)

citizenship (SIH•tuh•zuhn•ship): the way a person acts as a good citizen (235)

clinic (KLIH•nik): a place where people who are ill or hurt can get help (224)

communicate (kuh•MYOO•nih•kayt): to talk to and listen to someone else (134, 150)

community (kuh•MYOO•nih•tee): a place where people live (222)

conflict (KAHN•flikt): a disagreement or an argument between people (52)

crosswalk (KRAWS•wawk): a place marked on a street where people can cross safely (114)

danger (DAYN•jer): something that makes you not safe (132)

dental hygienists (DENT•uhl hy•JEN•ists): people who help a dentist by cleaning teeth (57)

dentists (DEN•tihsts): people who take care of teeth (56)

digest (dy•JEST): to break down food so that the body can use it (12)

dinner (DIH•ner): the meal most people eat in the evening (70)

disease (dih•ZEEZ): illness spread by germs (152)

doctor (DAWK•ter): a person who helps people who are ill or hurt get well (225)

drugs (DRUHGZ): things that change the way the body works (168)

emergency (ee•MER•juhn•see): a time when help is needed right away (107)

energy (EN•er•jee): the power that your body needs to do things (12)

environment (en•VY•ruhn•muhnt): the land, water, and air around you (226)

exercise (EK•ser•syz): activity that makes your body work hard (88)

fairness (FAIR•nuhs): treating others the way you want them to treat you (101)

feelings (FEE•lingz): ways you feel about things; for example, happy, sad, afraid, or excited (188)

floss (FLAHS): a special kind of thread for cleaning between your teeth (50)

Food Guide Pyramid (FOOD GYD PIR•uh•mid): a chart that shows people how much of each kind of food to eat to stay healthy (67)

friend (FREND): someone you enjoy being with who is not a family member (194)

germs (JERMZ): tiny things that can make you ill (26)

goal (GOHL): something to work for (18)

good touch (GUD TUHCH): a touch that makes you feel good, such as a hug or a pat on the back (198)

grow (GROH): to become taller and heavier (8)

habit (HA•bit): something a person does over and over (172)

heart (HART): a muscle that pumps blood through your body (16)

honest (AH•nihst): truthful (21)

ill (IL): not well; sick (146)

legal (LEE•guhl): allowed by the law (170)

litter (LIH•ter): trash that is not put in the right place (228)

love (LUHV): a special feeling of caring (206)

lunch (LUHNCH): the meal most people eat in the middle of the day (70)

lungs (LUHNGZ): two parts of your body that pump air in and out of your body; they take what your body needs from the air (14)

medicines (MED•ih•suhnz): drugs that help people get well or stay healthy (166)

muscles (MUH•suhlz): body parts that help you move (11)

nurse (NERS): a person who helps a doctor care for people who are ill or hurt (224)

permanent teeth (PER•muh•nuhnt TEETH): your second set of teeth, which you get after your primary teeth fall out (47)

physical fitness (FIZ•ih•kuhl FIT•nuhs): having a strong and healthy body (88)

playground equipment (PLAY•grownd ih•KWIP•muhnt): swings, slides, climbing bars, and other things on a playground (109)

poison (POY•zuhn): something that can make you sick if you swallow it or breathe it (136)

polite (puh•LYT): showing respect for others (199)

pollution (puh•LOO•shuhn): waste that harms the environment (226)

posture (PAHS•cher): the way you hold your body when you stand, sit, or move (86)

primary teeth (PRY•mair•ee TEETH): your baby teeth, the first set of teeth you get (46)

recycle (ree•SY•kuhl): to turn used things into new things (232)

refuse (rih•FYOOZ): to say NO to someone or something (176)

respect (rih•SPEKT): polite treatment of others (196)

responsibility (rih•spahn•suh•BIL•uh•tee): something you need because it is right and important (59)

responsible (rih•SPAHN•suh•buhl): able to be trusted to do the right thing (127)

safety belt (SAYF•tee BELT): a strap that holds you safely in your seat (110)

senses (SEN•suhz): the five ways your body helps you find out about the world—touch, sight, hearing, smell, and taste (4)

skeleton (SKEL•uh•tuhn): the bones of your body (10)

snack (SNAK): food you eat to give you energy between meals (72)

special (SPEH•shuhl): different from all others (186)

stranger (STRAYN•jer): someone you do not know (132)

stress (STRES): a way the body reacts to strong feelings (92, 192)

stretch (STRECH): to gently pull your muscles as a way to warm up and cool down before and after exercise (94)

sunburn (SUHN•bern): a burn of the skin caused by the sun's rays (28)

sunscreen (SUHN•skreen): a product that protects your skin from the sun (28)

tobacco (tuh•BAK•oh): dried plant leaves that contain drugs; they are smoked in cigarettes, cigars, and pipes or chewed in chewing tobacco (172)

tobacco smoke (tuh•BAK•oh SMOK): smoke from burning tobacco; it contains drugs and is harmful to people who breathe it (173)

vaccines (vak•SEENZ): medicines that keep people from getting certain diseases (154)

viruses (VY•ruhs•uhz): a kind of germ (153)

weapons (WEP•uhnz): things that can be used to hurt others (138)

Index

E

F

CREDITS